The French
Empire Style

The French Empire Style

Alvar Gonzalez-Palacios

HAMLYN

Translated by Raymond Rudorff from the Italian original

Dal Direttorio all'Impero

©*1966 Fratelli Fabbri Editori, Milan*

This edition © *copyright 1970*
THE HAMLYN PUBLISHING GROUP LIMITED
LONDON · NEW YORK · SYDNEY · TORONTO
Hamlyn House, Feltham, Middlesex, England

ISBN 0 600 01245 x

Text filmset by Filmtype Services, Scarborough, England

Printed in Italy by Fratelli Fabbri Editori, Milan

Bound in Scotland by Hunter and Foulis Ltd., Edinburgh

Contents

INTRODUCTION

'Without being a fanatical admirer of this style I still felt a sense of exultation at such grandiose proportions, such majesty of columns and such simple elegance of furniture and tapestries.' These words were written by the art historian Bernard Berenson, who was commenting, with his habitual and inimitable perspicacity, on the interior of the palace of Capodimonte at Naples, which is furnished in the Empire style. As usual, he found the *mots justes* to define the prime characteristics of the age: 'majesty' and 'grandiose'.

These were precisely the characteristics that Napoleon wished to see predominate in the decoration of the many palaces in his immense Empire. At all costs they had to be grandiose and majestic in order to proclaim his Olympian power throughout Europe. A son of the French Revolution, he nevertheless wished to emulate the 'Sun King' (Louis XIV) in splendour and magnificence; the same ambivalent attitude which made him wish to become a Moslem in Egypt, the defender of his country and its revolutionary principles under the Republic, and absolute dictator in his own Empire, led him to assume the pomp of the Bourbons and a rather theatrical air of grandeur, and show great astuteness by inviting the finest French artists into his services. With the same highly calculated nonchalance, he even scandalised his marshals by conferring the order of the Iron Crown on one of the most famous sopranos of all time, the castrato Crescentini. It is worth quoting the ugly but by no means unjust lines which brought imprisonment to

Desorgues, a minor poet of the time who showed scant deference to the Emperor:

Oui, le grand Napoléon
Est un grand camaléon
(Yes, the great Napoleon
Has become a great chameleon)

But this great chameleon went even further than Louis XIV, and perhaps even further than Louis XV, in his desire to surround himself with artists able to broadcast his glory *Urbi et Orbi*. The art of the first fifteen years of the 19th century was entirely centred on the Napoleonic deity, and is often impossible to understand if we do not bear in mind its initial inspiration. For example, how can David's paintings be explained without Napoleon? Every painting and every object seems intended to celebrate his glory. He was able to direct everything to this end with unfailing confidence, exiling those who, like Madame de Staël refused to submit to his dictates, and flattering, bribing and threatening. Is there a single effigy or portrait-type of Louis XVI or any other 18th-century sovereign which immediately springs to mind? I do not believe there is. But anyone with the slightest acquaintance with history rather than art will immediately have a mental image of the features of Augustus, Alexander or Charles V. The 'French Caesar' wished to join these immortals, and therefore had himself portrayed in paint, marble and bronze. He almost never had to pose in person, for he was idealised like some pagan god or emperor in portraits which proclaimed his identity at the first glance.

The society of the Empire was quite different from

that of the feverish, rhetorical and somewhat confused *bohème* of the first post-Revolutionary period. The time had passed when ladies were content to wear a piece of stone from the Bastille, set in a simple silver mounting, around their necks. They now wanted more sumptuous jewellery, and the Emperor himself wore the gigantic 'Regent' diamond for his own apotheosis – his coronation. Not content with kidnapping the Pope for this solemn ceremony, he even wanted him to play a gentle, consecrating role while Napoleon placed the imperial crown upon his own head. It was hardly surprising, in view of all this display, that General Delmas left after making the terrible remark: 'A fine flummery! A pity the hundred thousand men who got killed to put an end to all this are not still here!' But such soldiers had long disappeared, and were spared the scandalous sight of Laetitia Ramolino's sons becoming princes and kings, and their old comrades-in-arms becoming barons and marshals. These new men were no longer content with the delicate harmonies of Directoire interiors, with their clear liquid pastel tints; what they now wanted was gold, gaudy decoration, triumphal furnishings with bronze *parures,* and all the solid, warlike pomp of soldiers who had become men of wealth.

This new demand was met by two near-geniuses who satisfied the aspirations to glory of this society – which wished to ape Classical antiquity not from love of stoic simplicity but because it hoped thereby to justify its own idiosyncrasies. Charles Percier (1764-1838) and Pierre Fontaine (1762-1853) became the despots of French interior decoration. Even more remarkable, their work was without the excessive celebratory emphasis that characterises so much of the art and craftsmanship of the period. It was free from the extraordinary conceptions of a Ledoux or the stupendous abstract lucubrations of a Boullée (two architects whose projects heralded the poetic ideals of the Empire style), but there was much grace in their exquisite furniture designs and in their grandiose yet intimate decorations. Sometimes, it is true, their art trod a razor's edge: too many chimeras, too many winged lions and too many wild beasts' claws cluttered up the linear design of a chair, but only occasionally. They would make such works as incense burners which retained all the enchantment of Hellenistic art, or symbolic friezes which showed surprising lightness of touch, with allusions to the occupant of the room for which they were designed.

Empire art teemed with symbols. The room of the painter Isabey was decorated with allegorical figures of the art; a library would be decorated with portraits of the greatest writers of all ages; a soldier would have lances and shields painted on his walls or inlaid in his doors. Egyptomania was everywhere triumphant. Thirty years before, the Italian Piranesi, who made such a decisive contribution to the evolution of the Neo-Classical style, had published his *Diverse maniere d'adornare i camini* (Different ways of decorating fireplaces) (1769), in which many Egyptian motifs made their appearance; but it was Napoleon's triumphal sojourn in Egypt that led to a frenzied enthusiasm for Egyptian art. A piece of furniture, a clock or an ink-stand became a pretext for portraying

1   Jacques-Louis David (1748-1825). *The Coronation of Napoleon*. (detail). Louvre, Paris.

1   Jacques-Louis David (1748-1825). *The Coronation of Napoleon*. (detail). Louvre, Paris. This was painted between 1805 and 1808, and shows a certain deference on David's part to colour values. In the detail reproduced are some of the master's greatest portraits, each one composed with an abstract self-sufficiency reminiscent, in a more heroic manner, of Chekov's personages.

2   Pierre Prud'hon (1758-1823). *Portrait of the Empress Josephine*. Louvre, Paris. The poetic composition and the way in which the figure reclines gracefully against a vague, shady landscape, make this one of the most elegant portraits of the period. It dates from 1805, and shows the artist's skill in landscape painting at its most pleasing.

3   François Gérard (1770-1837). *Psyche Receiving the First Kiss of Love*. Louvre, Paris. A graceful, light-filled and airy composition of 1798. In its languid, glacial lyricism it has affinities with Boizot's or Brachard's Sèvres figurines and the same sense of gracious necrophilia tinged with a pure, sharp voluptuousness.

4   Jacques-Louis David (1748-1825). *Portrait of Madame Récamier*. Louvre, Paris. By elegantly draping the clearly modelled and statuesque body of Madame Récamier, reclining with studied grace on her Directoire *méridienne*, David was aiming to create a type which would epitomise female beauty of the period. The portrait was never completed and was painted with Ingres' help in 1800.

2   Pierre Prud'hon (1758-1823). *Portrait of the Empress Josephine*. Louvre, Paris.

3   François Gérard (1770-1837). *Psyche Receiving the First Kiss of Love*. Louvre, Paris.

4   Jacques-Louis David (1748-1825). *Portrait of Madame Récamier*. Louvre, Paris.

as many Egyptian divinities as possible, in works with such titles as 'Nature in the form of Osiris'. Sometimes there was a *mélange*, as when artists mixed up Egyptian sphinxes or confounded Greek gryphons with the monsters of Egypt. But all previous limits were surpassed when the Emperor decided to have an enormous table-piece made at Sèvres in biscuit porcelain, in the form of a kind of ideal anthology of Egyptian architecture.

A major contribution to this Egyptian style was made by the Baron Dominique Vivant Denon (1745-1825), who had been an impassioned collector of Etruscan vases before becoming an enthusiastic Egyptologist, publishing his famous *Voyage dans la Basse et Haute Egypte pendant les campagnes du Général Bonaparte* in 1802. The engravings illustrating this learned work immediately became an inexhaustible pattern-book for the foremost interior decorators of the day, and the book went through numerous editions in various languages. Denon was the first to evince a desire for Egyptian furniture in his own home and made an accurate drawing of the grandiose portico of Ghoos so that Biennais might reproduce it in mahogany and silver for a coin-cabinet.

But the threatening wild beasts of Egypt and Rome were not the only motifs to triumph in Napoleonic interiors, for the hard edges of commodes and armchairs were softened by the heraldic sign of the swan in milk-white tints of lustre of gold, and its silky plumage caressed the cold sheen of the finest silks. The motif first appeared on Madame Récamier's bed in

1798 and was to remain in France until the swan had become old and featherless under the Restoration, when it was henceforth relegated to the attic. An almost equally tragic fate overtook the fountain designed by Thomire. It was to be crowned by an enormous bronze elephant carved by the famous craftsman, and was to stand on the site of the former Bastille. In 1811 a twenty-four-metre-high model was built and set up on the chosen site. But the following year the disastrous Russian campaign took place, and the authorities had other things to think about than Thomire's fountain. As the years passed, the enormous wooden elephant continued to preside in majesty over the site of the former royal prison – until 1846, when the decision was taken to demolish it, since it had simply become a ruin and an obstacle. No sooner had the first pick axe blows split open the carcass of the elephant than thousands of large moles came running out of it in terror, invading the entire district . . . *Sic transit gloria mundi.*

PAINTING

Jacques-Louis David
In the twenty-three years that elapsed between the fall of the guillotine blade that killed Louis XVI and the famous defeat that put an end to Napoleon's sensational career, French painting was dominated by the singular and contradictory personality of Jacques-Louis David. His contribution to what has been called the 'Revolutionary style' is well known. For examples

it is only necessary to cite the paintings he executed in the last years of the monarchy, beginning with his *Brutus* of 1789, which was almost a declaration of principles and a manifesto proclaiming man's duties towards his homeland. Immediately afterwards David joined the extreme left wing of the revolutionaries, becoming a fervent disciple of Robespierre. It became his task to prepare the programmes – filled with obscure moralistic-philosophical symbols – for every patriotic anniversary and revolutionary procession, thus continuing in a way that worship of great men which was a constant of late 18th-century art. He was an indefatigable worker, and his activities ranged from projects for 'citizens' dwellings to sketches and studies for *The Tennis Court Oath*, a splendid pictorial pamphlet which was never completed but which remains a striking work on account of its grandiose spatial sense and the novelty and passion of the composition. The death of Lepeletier gave David the opportunity to commemorate one of the first victims of the Counter-Revolution in an extremely original composition which is known only through a contemporary engraving, since the work was destroyed – perhaps by his daughter. Soon afterwards, with his *Death of Marat* (1793, Musées Royaux des Beaux-Arts, Brussels), David revolutionised modern painting and modern sensibility. The painting is of modest dimensions, the colouring is harsh and almost stoic in the sobriety of its technique. The tribune, idealised as though he were a pagan hero, lies in a state of livid nudity, surrounded by humble objects all miraculously caught in an almost hallucinatory light. With its anti-

5　Antoine-Jean Gros (1771-1835). *Bonaparte Visiting the Plague-Stricken Soldiers in the Hospital at Jaffa on March 11th 1799*. Louvre, Paris.

6   Jean-Auguste-Dominique Ingres (1780-1867). *Madame
Destouches*. Louvre, Paris.

7　Jean-Auguste-Dominique Ingres (1780-1867). *Portrait of Madame Devauçay*. Musée Condé, Chantilly.

5   Antoine-Jean Gros (1771-1835). *Bonaparte Visiting the Plague-Stricken Soldiers in the Hospital at Jaffa on March 11th 1799.* Louvre, Paris. Gros was a pupil of David, and Delacroix's ideal master. In this composition, dating from 1804, he already showed a Romantic predilection for the exotic. Napoleon's gesture is similar to that of the doubting Saint Thomas in many Italian paintings.

6   Jean-Auguste-Dominique Ingres (1780-1867). *Madame Destouches.* Cabinet des Estampes. Louvre, Paris. The drawings of Ingres are among the most perfect in the history of art; he himself declared that 'drawing is the probity of art'. This portrait, dating from 1816, already shows an enchanting hint of Neo-Gothic intimacy.

7   Jean-Auguste-Dominique Ingres (1780-1867). *Portrait of Madame Devauçay.* Musée Condé, Chantilly. Every detail in the painting is evidence of that meticulous abstract realism which justified Gautier's judgement that 'Ingres is in no way Classical'. The work is signed and dated 1807.

8   Jean-Auguste-Dominique Ingres (1780-1867). *Raphael's House at Rome.* Musée des Arts Décoratifs, Paris. Standing half-way between the landscapes of Poussin and those of the young Corot, this view resembles some of the landscape backgrounds in the portraits of Ingres' early Roman period, like those of the painter Granet.

9   Anne-Louis Girodet (1767-1824). *The Shades of the French Warriors led by Victory into Odin's Palace, being received by the Homer of the North and the warlike phantoms of Fingal and his descendants.* Louvre, Paris. Painted in 1801 to satisfy the tastes of the First Consul, an avid reader of Ossian, the original composition was made by Percier and Fontaine at Malmaison.

8   Jean-Auguste-Dominique Ingres (1780-1867).
Raphael's House at Rome. Musée des Arts Décoratifs, Paris.

9 Anne-Louis Girodet (1767-1824). *The Shades of the French Warriors led by Victory into Odin's Palace*. Louvre, Paris.

rhetorical, basic naturalism and its simplicity of emotion the painting is almost a secular *Pietà*, and a kind of modern saint's icon with the martyr – the friend of the people and victim of tyranny – shown almost as a new St Peter the Martyr. It is almost as though the painter were saying 'here is his corpse and the knife that killed him: pray for him and know that he is in heaven (or better still, by the side of the goddess Reason) watching over you all.' In works such as this, filled with implicit political meanings, David attained a degree of poetic force beyond the reach of any other artist then living in Europe, with the possible exception of the great Canova.

. But his pictorial career was far from concluded with this work. Once the Utopian dreams of the Jacobins, with whom David had been so closely linked, had been drowned in blood, it was as though David became temporarily enclosed in himself, concentrating on the Greek ideal of abstract beauty which had always profoundly influenced him. The result of the long and patient studies of these years was the resoundingly successful monumental painting, *The Sabine Women* (in the Louvre), which he completed in 1799. Many spectators have perhaps remained unmoved by the exquisite modelling of the statuesque bodies, the deliberately sober colouring, free from all hedonistic undertones, the severely Classical landscape, and the striking unreality of the action, in which space and time seem to have dissolved, giving way to a kind of theatrical display of splendid wax figures. The discerning and unprejudiced spectator will see that this marble-like tableau has a life of its own and reveals the captivating power of limitless and genuinely pictorial compositional solutions. We should not speak of affectation and 'iciness' in the work of David, or let ourselves be misled by the limits imposed by present day taste when attempting to appreciate works of the past. Simone Martini's work might just as well be called 'frozen', for it is as 'unreal' as that of David. The creamy consistency of Fragonard's nudes may perhaps be regarded as more 'truthful' than David's difficult idealised figures, but in art truth is a matter of complex design, and should not be confused with mere verisimilitude.

David was able to paint in the most effectively realistic vein on certain occasions, as in two of his finest portraits, *Comte François de Nantes* (1811, Musée Jacquemart-André, Paris) and *Monsieur et Madame de Mongez* (1812, Louvre, Paris). They display a psychological insight which could only stem from the painter's capacity for acute observation and his intuitive grasp of the essence of a character. Quite different in spirit is his unfinished portrait of the famous muse of the day, Madame Récamier, shown reclining provokingly in her thin flowing dress and even more complacently aware of her own charms than Canova's Pauline Borghese, despite the latter's self-possessed nudity. These two women were to remain prototypes for feminine beauty in the early 19th century. It is tempting to ask whether voluptuousness was unimaginable at this time without a chaise-longue, so much did this graceful piece of furniture seem an essential adjunct to the erotic appeal of these two famous practitioners of the *ars amandi* during the exuberant, uninhibited years of the French Empire.

In his portrait of Madame Récamier David created a 'type' for all time by idealising a certain conception of the 'eternal woman'. After 1800, the year of the painting, Bonaparte's star began to glow with ever-increasing brilliance in the European firmament. David then lost his head completely, and forgetting what he had said after the death of Robespierre ('I shall no longer attach myself to men, only to principles'), found the incarnation of his hero in the young Napoleon. Five years later, when he had become 'Napoleonis francorum imperatoris primarius pictor', as he signed himself in his stupendous portrait of Pius VII (Louvre), he painted the enormous canvas of *The Coronation of Napoleon,* which now dominates one of the largest rooms in the Louvre. When we compare it with *The Sabine Women* painted only a few years before, we cannot help being struck by the change in David's technique. Whereas the earlier work seems cold, deliberately restrained and artificial, the *Coronation* has all the exuberant warm colouring of a Rubens and, in its explosive virtuosity, affinities with some of Goya's works and the impassioned Romanticism of Delacroix. Rather than indulge in an analysis of David's intelligent composition, by which he represented the sumptuous splendour of the ceremony without any rhetorical exaltation of the central figures and skilfully avoided any hint of vulgarity or conventionality, the author would like to draw attention to the subtle and imaginative use of colour in every face, in every embroidered costume and in every gold thread, and to the extraordinary way in which every figure is made to participate in the action. David, as remarked, had become Napoleon's first painter, and the attentive historian and enthusiastic narrator of his every deed, as we may see from the other great painting, *The Distribution of the Eagles* (1810, Musée de Versailles), and numerous similar subjects which remained in sketch-books in his studio. The most faithful images David left to posterity are perhaps those which concern Napoleon himself and dwell upon the essence of the man. Among such works are the various versions of the famous *Napoleon crossing the Saint Bernard Pass* in which Bonaparte is depicted 'serene upon a fiery horse' as the general had himself asked David to portray him, adding that 'it is not with the sword that battles are won'. Less known but even more intimate and convincing is *Napoleon in his study* (1810, National Gallery, Washington), in which David caught an instant in the private life of an emperor. He painted him being interrupted during his nocturnal labours – the clock shows thirteen minutes past four and a candle is softly glowing in the *lampe-bouillotte* – rising pale and weary from his leather upholstered arm-chair and his splendid writing table with legs in the shape of winged lions (which must certainly have been the work of Jacob-Desmalter). David had attentively observed every object in the room and represented them with a kind of detached, phlegmatic narrative candour, as though to immortalise the exact topography of the room as much as the man himself.

There is no need to follow David's career after his exile to Brussels, where he decided to settle since,

10   Charles-Louis Corbet (1758-1808). *Bust of General Bonaparte*. Musée de l'Armée aux Invalides, Paris.

11   Joseph Chinard (1756-1813). *Young Woman with Cockaded Cap*. Musée Carnavalet, Paris.

12   Paolo Triscornia (died 1832). *Bust of Marie-Louise*.
Versailles.

10 Charles-Louis Corbet (1758-1808). *Bust of General Bonaparte.* Musée de l'Armée aux Invalides, Paris. This beautiful portrait, which was one of the artist's masterpieces, shows the young Bonaparte at the time of his military triumphs in Italy. The gesso model in the Invalides has been reproduced instead of the slightly more conventional marble bust.

11 Joseph Chinard (1756-1813). *Young Woman with Cockaded Cap.* Musée Carnavalet, Paris. A graceful little portrait, modelled by Chinard in the Revolutionary period, which still bears traces of the 18th-century style despite its obviously patriotic inspiration. The assurance in which the effigy of the young woman has been set within the round medallion is noteworthy.

12 Paolo Triscornia (died 1832). *Bust of Marie-Louise.* Versailles. Triscornia also worked at Saint Petersburg. His sculpture followed the precepts of the Empire style with skill but great coldness.

13 Jean-Antoine Houdon (1741-1828). *Bust of Napoleon.* Musée des Beaux-Arts, Dijon. Without a doubt, the most accomplished work of the artist's last period. A successful blend of realism and abstraction, with the Classical features of the Emperor tinged with a Romantic emotion which in no way detracts from the humanity and magnanimity of the expression. The work is dated 1806.

13   Jean-Antoine Houdon (1741-1828). *Bust of Napoleon.*
Musée des Beaux-Arts, Dijon.

being an atheist, a regicide and a Bonapartist, he had refused to compromise his dignity by making any submission, even a purely formal one, to the restored Bourbon monarchy. After Waterloo his work declined but his presence was still influential, and many of his pupils, like Gros, continued to play an important role in art. That these artists were greatly indebted to David is not always admitted to-day; but at the time it was recognised by such painters as Delacroix and the rebellious Géricault.

François Gérard
Apart from David, what other painters distinguished themselves in that intense twenty years? First of all there were his pupils, beginning with Ingres, who all painted their own 'commentaries' on the work and ideas of the master. The author of numerous but insipid portraits of the new aristocracy, François Gérard (1770-1837) painted rather superficial but enchantingly chic portraits of the languid, elegant and fragile members of the imperial aristocracy in a manner which had affinities with that of the great English portraitists.

His works give the impression of being from the pages of a fashion journal with advertisements for the foremost tailors of the period. One of the personalities of the time that he portrayed was Madame Récamier; but instead of the discarnate sensuality with which David had invested her, he gave her only a perfumed charm and a more obvious, but more facile voluptuousness. Gérard could achieve convincing effects at times, as in the beautiful portrait of the painter Isabey with his little daughter (1795, Louvre). The skilfully distributed pale yellow light rising from the lower half of the canvas gives a romantic aura to the emaciated face of the young man, lighting up his elegant and close-fitting costume, painted with the confident precision of a dandy. The chaste, bloodless representation of *Cupid and Psyche* (1798, Louvre) is of a delicate antithesis between two naked and almost absurdly lifeless adolescents set in a complex geometrical composition against a landscape rendered with the exactitude of a transfer. This sugary, frivolous, vaporous little mythological subject has a certain funereal charm, as though the two young lovers had been rendered in death, with the graceful butterfly fluttering above their heads symbolising their souls in flight to some celestial domain. But Gérard's graceful bloodless creations were not to everyone's taste, if we are to believe the story that the sculptor Giraud maliciously asked himself whether Psyche's profile was rendered in length or in breadth. The present author willingly subscribes to the opinion of Friedländer, who wrote that 'in style and sentiment Gérard is essentially a painter of ladies'.

Anne-Louis Girodet

A somewhat different artist was Anne-Louis Girodet (1767-1824), a painter who had received a rich cultural training and was an avid reader of the early Romantics. The pupil of David and Gros, he rebelled against their teachings while continuing to be influenced by their power and truthfulness. He decided to break away from the stoic style of David as early as 1792 in his *Endymion* (Louvre), a work in which the Correggesque light and feminine nudity of the youth produce a rather embarassing effect of effeminate sensuality in a vein which is a far cry from the spirit of Classical art. All the works of this Alexandrian aesthete and man of letters (whom David called 'trop savant pour nous', 'too clever for us') lend themselves to caricature, although they contain certain important and original technical and pictorial innovations. His several versions of the *Danae* – the finest being that of 1800 in the Minneapolis Museum – feature a kind of complaisant and affected carnavalesque fancy-dress presented with humorous lasciviousness and an occasional hint of sadism. The paintings teem with peacocks' plumes, antique masks, precious mirrors, exotic turbans, crucified and tasselled doves, and even a malignant turkey with the features of the former lover of the protagonist – nothing is lacking in this incredible repertory. The 'sad, Catholic, romantic' composition of *The Burial of Atala* (1808, Louvre) would be better suited to the grand finale of Verdi's *Force of Destiny* than the mystical exaltation of Chateaubriand's story.

The painting commissioned by Napoleon (a fervid admirer of Ossian), *The Shades of the French Warriors in Odin's Palace* (1801, Malmaison, the sketch is in the Louvre), almost defies description. It is worth quoting Mario Praz's witty description of this painting, with its pretentious *personnages en cristal*: 'Instead of dressing up his French heroes in Classical robes, he puts them in as they are: marshals with

14   Geographical pendulum clock in Sèvres biscuit-porcelain. Musée Marmottan, Paris.

37

14 Geographical pendulum-clock in Sèvres biscuit-porcelain. Musée Marmottan, Paris. The clock was begun in 1813 and was to be crowned by a bust of Napoleon, but it was completed under the Restoration. The overall design was by Fragonard the younger. Develly painted the miniatures on the dial and Brachard supervised the execution of the carvings.

15 Porcelain ink-stand from the Dagoty factory. Malmaison. This enchanting object was made by one of the foremost Paris manufactories at the turn of the 18th century and proves that French porcelain of the highest quality was not confined to Sèvres. Dagoty was porcelain-maker to the Empress Josephine, and the work dates from about 1805.

16 Bronze clock with marble base. Malmaison. Clock-making became a pretext for making extremely decorative *objets d'art* such as this one with its representation of Jason carrying off the Golden Fleece. Note the exquisite execution of the bronze-work, which has been given an antique patina and gilded for greater ornamental effect. It dates from about 1800.

15 Porcelain ink-stand from the Dagoty factory.
Malmaison.

braided uniforms and curved sabres, grenadiers with high fur helmets and the occasional pipe smoking under their bushy moustaches, in an assembly of epic warriors with hoary beards and flaming eyes with a chorus of ministering nymphs floating in a vaporous paradise to offer goblets and garlands to the new arrivals and flatter their ears with the strains of their harps; a great black eagle hovering in apotheosis against the clouds and a young dragoon with the sword of honour given him by the First Consul killing the ferocious Starno, King of Loclin and Fingal's enemy.'

Pierre-Narcisse Guérin
Pierre-Narcisse Guérin (1774-1833) also made a bid for fame with his *Return of Marcus Sextus* (Louvre), a painting which obtained such a clamorous success in 1799 that it was hailed by David's opponents as a rival to his own far more genuine creations. The work had a certain theatrical effectiveness and was composed in a style derived from the *Brutus* and other pre-Revolutionary paintings of David; but it suffered from a fundamental lack of truthfulness, and the deliberately solemn theme was weakened by a gratuitous rhetoric. What probably contributed to the immediate success of the painting was its implicit political content, for it did not require overmuch imagination on the part of the spectator to draw a parallel between the *émigrés* who were about to return to France and the tragic banishment of Sextus, shown stepping across the threshold of his house just in time to behold his dead wife and heart-broken

daughter. It cannot be said that Guérin lacked expressive power; he had profited from the lessons of David and those of his master Regnault, a painter now mainly remembered by his *Three Graces* in the Louvre (1799). But Guérin lacked the powerful imagination of the true creative artist. The best of his works, such as the *Phaedra and Hippolytus* (1802), *Cupid and Cephalus* (1810), *Dido and Aeneas* (1813) and *Clytemnestra* (1817), now all in the Louvre, or the *Morpheu and Iris* in the Hermitage, merely confirm his undoubted gifts as a skilful stage-manager. (Their virtuoso choreographic effects were partly inspired by the productions of the Comédie Française, and partly by the most successful interior designs of Percier and Fontaine.) But a consummate technique and a rich repertory of exquisite stage props – antique-style beds with gilded bronze, leopard skins, purple hangings – do not suffice to make his paintings works of art even though they are handled with great intellectual sophistication.

Antoine-Jean Gros
Antoine-Jean Gros (1771-1835), David's favourite pupil, worked in a more varied style and was undoubtedly more talented. The artist's personality was dominated by two opposing tendencies for although he was instinctively drawn towards a richly-coloured, vital and avant-garde form of painting, he could not break away from the influence of David's idealistic style and was infatuated by David's theoretical conceptions. It is obvious that his most significant works are those in which rich emotional colouring and

heartfelt human pathos have the upper hand over preconceived intellectual ideas, as in his most important painting, in which he portrayed Napoleon with what Delacroix called 'a rare blend of force and elegance'. The great *Bonaparte Visiting the Plague-Stricken Soldiers at Jaffa,* painted in 1804 and exhibited at the Salon of the same year, is a triumph of colour and might be a homage to Rubens and certain aspects of the Italian Baroque. Gros had stayed for a long time contemplating Rubens' paintings at Genoa, and his work was almost entirely free from any suggestion of David's style. It is worth mentioning that scarcely a year later, as he began work on *The Coronation of Napoleon,* David himself felt the need to study the Rubens paintings commissioned by Marie de' Medici, and that in his youth he had made a long study of the works of Caravaggio's followers, whose influence could be detected in his *Saint Roch* at Marseille. There is, however, no doubt that the *Plague-Stricken Soldiers at Jaffa* inaugurated a new way of painting which was in part based on the precepts of Neo-Classicism but which broke away from perfect geometry in order to allow the artist freedom in the placing of his figures, and which came to depend increasingly on rich, lively brushwork. The definition of 'Romantic Classicism' made by certain critics seems particularly applicable to Gros' work, which stands halfway between David's pondered idealism and Delacroix's impassioned vigour. The figure of the nude bearded man kneeling on the right of the picture is of the same type as the plague-stricken sufferer that David painted in his *Saint Roch* at Marseille and the figure that Delacroix painted with corrections and alterations in his *Massacre of Chios*. As for Gros' vibrant, rich colouring, it is worth quoting the verses that Girodet dedicated to him:

> O Gros! où trouvas-tu cette teinte éclatante
> Qu'offre à l'oeil ébloui ta palette brulante?
> Emule heureux de Paul, rival de Titien,
> Leur immense talent est devenue le tien.
> (Oh Gros! where did you find those flaming hues
> That your burning palette presents to the dazzled eye that views?
> Happy disciple of Paul and rival of Titian,
> Their immense talent has become your own)

Their representation of Napoleon is one of great originality: he is here depicted as a kind of supernatural, beneficent, healing deity, about to work miracles and pale as a saint in the face of death. Without sacrificing the dignity of his art, Gros had succeeded in finding the right way to publicise his hero in a convincing manner.

A few years later, in his excellent *Napoleon at Eylau* (1808, Louvre), he showed the Emperor in the guise of a mild and magnanimous conqueror; but the portrait contains a hint of the coming *débâcle*. In spirit the work is far removed from the Napoleon-Zeus of the young Ingres, the triumphant *basileus* of David and even from Gros' own miraculous healer of the plague-stricken. Napoleon is depicted as the man of remission, with livid, exhausted features and profound, sad eyes, seated high on his charger in exotic Oriental costume (a detail that was to be taken up

17 Mahogany candlesticks. Praz Collection, Rome. The two candlesticks carved as 'two Egyptian water-carriers in exquisitely carved mahogany, with their gilded bronze amphora serving as candle-holders' are a great rarity, since such objects were usually made in bronze during the Empire period.

18 Detail of the Sèvres Egyptian table piece. The Duke of Wellington Collection, Reading. Made under the direct supervision of Vivant Denon, it consists of exact reconstructions of various Egyptian temples. It was made for the Emperor, who wished to give it as a present to the Tsar after the Peace of Tilsit.

19 Plate in Paris porcelain. Sèvres Museum. The plate is decorated with an anticipated portrait of the King of Rome, who had not yet been born. This sublime piece of courtly flattery was offered to the Emperor by the porcelain manufacturers Dihl and Guerhard, in 1810. The plate measures ten inches across.

20 Plate in Sèvres porcelain. Malmaison. During the Empire, the Sèvres factory devoted itself entirely to the production of hard paste porcelain with a kaolin base, since it was particularly suitable for obtaining the effects of light and the impeccable finish that were then in vogue. The plate dates from 1805.

18   Detail of Egyptian table-piece of Sèvres ware. The
Duke of Wellington Collection, Reading.

19 Plate in Paris porcelain. Sèvres Museum.

20   Plate in Sèvres porcelain. Malmaison.

again later by the artists of the Romantic Movement).

An equally unexpected artistic originality led Gros to execute portraits in the most varied styles. His manner was virile and Goyaesque in his portrait of Colonel Fournier (1812, Louvre), surrounded by an aura of glowing brush-strokes; and that of a languid, delicate *poseur* in his posthumous portrait of Christine Boyer, Lucien Bonaparte's first wife (1812, Louvre), with her arms artistically folded, standing in an attitude of melancholy meditation by the silky waters of a stream in which she had just let fall a withered rose. It was perhaps the same gloomy, restless melancholy which led the artist to make that most romantic of gestures by committing suicide in 1835.

Pierre Prud'hon

The art of Pierre Prud'hon (1758-1823) is more difficult to classify, for it relates to no one specific tendency. The French Correggio, as he was called, seemed to flee from all contact with the style of the time, and from the severe examples of Neo-Classical art which had begun to manifest themselves in the 1780s. He preferred the favourite themes of the 18th century, dwelling upon them in a spirit of happy sensuality. Neither the wars nor the artistic polemics of the period shattered the tranquility of his enclosed garden of the imagination, in which the nude figures of Psyche and Zephyr, veiled only in the mauve of the evening mist, leaned enchanted over the water against a background of mossy rocks and drooping plants lit by the dreamlike rays of the moon. Any lady that strayed into his garden also became veiled in the same exquisite aura, like his Josephine gracefully draped in the winding folds of her kashmir shawl. Prud'hon was capable of painting a nude with a solidity and precision that would not have displeased Géricault; for instance the figure of the young victim in *Justice and Revenge pursuing Crime* (1808, Louvre). He could move the spectator with the sight of human suffering too, as in his *Crucifixion* (1822, Louvre), which has an intensity worthy of Delacroix despite its different style. But this was not where the true genius of this lyrical Robespierre *avec grâce* lay, for he was always attracted by the charm of his own personal twilight world of soft shadows. 'He is mistaken', David said of him, 'but it is not given to everyone to be mistaken as he is.'

Jean-Auguste-Dominique Ingres
'All painting lies in strong and fine drawing together. Whatever people may say, it is only to be found in a firm drawing with proud character, even in a picture which must impress by its grace. Grace alone is not enough, nor is restrained drawing. Far more is needed: the drawing must amplify, it must surround everything . . . Drawing is also the expression, the inner form, the plan and the modelling. Drawing constitutes three-and-a-half quarters of painting.' Given the iron principles which lay behind their creation, it is not surprising that the paintings of Jean-Auguste-Dominique Ingres (1780-1867) attained that degree of Olympian serenity which enchants all who study the art of the period. Despite the appearance of an objective idealism, his art reveals attentive

study of every single linear and chromatic detail and an obsessive concentration on every aspect of a face or figure; so that when examined more closely his style displays an unsuspected and nervous restlessness. So striking are these qualities that it is tempting to ignore his obstinate idolatry of the 'divine Raphael' and the faith he proclaimed in the apostolic purity of art, which he passionately believed to be a high and sacerdotal moral mission. The fact that it is dangerous to make any brief assessment of Ingres' singular and rich contribution to the history of art was already recognised by Baudelaire who, with customary perspicacity, observed: 'The works of Ingres, which are the result of excessive study, demand equal study to be understood.'

Ingres was trained according to David's precepts and by the beginning of the century was already entrusted with work on the marginal details of David's portrait of Madame Récamier. A short time later, when he may have been in close contact with the strange group of dissident artists known as the Primitifs or Barbus, he broke away for ever from David's school; he preferred to pursue his own paradoxical study of 'Primitivism', founded on the study of 'Etruscan' vases whose compact, clear-cut linear rhythms had fascinated the bearded followers of the rebel school. The result of his studies were works like the *Venus wounded by Diomedes* (Von Hirsch Collection) in which linear simplification of planes is offset by a greater sense of volume.

In *Oedipus and the Sphinx* (1808, Louvre), a subject of which Ingres left many variants in his obsessive

21   Tea cup in Sèvres porcelain. Musée Carnavalet, Paris.

21   Tea cup in Sèvres porcelain. Musée Carnavalet, Paris. After the fall of the monarchy, some Sèvres ware declined greatly in quality; but some pieces, such as this elegant cup, simply substituted Republican symbols for the previous flower patterns.

22   Sugar bowl in Sèvres porcelain. The Duke of Wellington Collection, Reading. Part of the same table service as the piece in plate 18. The sugar bowl is painted in blue and gold and is decorated with illegible hieroglyphics directly inspired by those on ancient monuments. The bowl dates from about 1810.

23   Pierre-Philippe Thomire (1751-1843). Bronze candle-holder. Malmaison. A splendid branched candlestick featuring a winged Victory who holds a laurel wreath supporting the candle-holders. A work in the full Empire style. Notice the extraordinary quality of the execution and the beautiful colour effect given by the contrast between the gilt and the patina.

24   Oil lamp. Musée des Arts Décoratifs, Paris. Even such modest objects as this oil lamp, of the type known as *quinquet,* were inspired by the Classical style and attained the dignity of works of art. The lamp, made of plain tin and varnished bronze, dates from about 1800.

22   Sugar bowl in Sèvres porcelain. The Duke of Wellington Collection, Reading.

23 Pierre-Philippe Thomire (1751-1843). Bronze candle-
holder. Malmaison.

24   Oil lamp. Musée des Arts Décoratifs, Paris.

desire for perfection, can be seen examples of this grafting of Classical form on to a Romantic content, which some critics regard – perhaps rightly – as a peculiar characteristic of Ingres' art. In some of these displays of 'Gothicism', as contemporaries regarded them, many 'Romantic' features were effectively present in his works, inserted within the context of an impeccable formal manner which sought to conceal the presence of the craftsman by its Apollian perfection. Often it was the subjects themselves which explicitly revealed a Neo-Gothic taste: *Raphael and the Fornarina*; the Oriental odalisques who appeared in several paintings culminating in the famous *Bain Turc* of 1863, a sublime anthology of voluptuousness and repressed desires which brilliantly concluded the artist's career at the age of eighty-three; and the series of episodes of modern European history seen from a pseudo-historical 18th-century viewpoint. Of all his historical paintings, the most extreme example of Ingres' peculiar brand of Romanticism was the *Dream of Ossian* (Musée Ingres, Montauban), which he painted in 1813 for Napoleon's bed-chamber in the Quirinal. What David thought of these translucid, ethereal and weightless figures, has not been recorded. Certainly they were a far cry from his *personnages en cristal!* Looking at them it is easy to understand why someone once defined Ingres as a 'Chinaman in Greece'.

Of all the aspects of his artistic production, the most famous and – in the opinion of many, though not of the painter himself – the most successful, were the portraits. In 1804, having painted his own portrait after a long study of his face in a mirror, Ingres began a splendid series of portraits in which he rendered every state of the soul and every stirring of the emotions painstakingly and with seeming objectivity. Unlike David's sublime idealisations in which people became abstract entities in some inaccessible empyrean, and in which objects were granted a purely symbolic existence, Ingres aimed at a greater effect of intimacy, concentrating on a psychological investigation which may have not been as total but which was just as intense. Whereas David aimed at portraying a human type, Ingres searched for the truth in each individual who was surrounded by real objects rendered with every detail that could bring out their significance. By means of a refined stylisation and close attention to every single detail, he produced the series of hallucinatory portraits of the Rivières, Madame Devauçay, *La Belle Zelie*, the painter Grante and the horrid Madame de Tournon. They all have a powerful though serene presence, rivalling the most lifelike characters of Flaubert, Balzac and Proust. In creating this extraordinary gallery of portraits, in which a whole society showed itself in its most varied aspects without ever revealing all its innermost secrets, Ingres was unable to make use of the spoken word, which could have re-created surroundings, deeds and circumstances in a flash. He was obliged to depend on a single image to depict the essence of a life, one significant detail to symbolise each entelechy; and, as Baudelaire pointed out, part of the total effect of the portrait depends on the spectator's own interpretation of it. Ingres was thus able to attain his aims without any need for a personal intervention which would have diminished the intensity and versimilitude of his works, and it is in this that the true grandeur of his art lay.

SCULPTURE

The sculptors of the Empire period produced works in abundance but in creative vigour they were far inferior to the great painters of the age. This was not because sculptors lacked state patronage, for they also worked in privileged conditions; but there was no great outstanding personality among them of the stature of Gros, David or Ingres. Not even the use of colour could give life to their imitative and all too often pedestrian imitations of antique sculpture, which no longer had the charm of the Louis XVI statuary in which elegant Neo-Classical stylisation was combined with impassioned study of the human figure. The works of Joseph Chinard (1756-1813), perhaps the most talented of Empire sculptors, did not rise above the level of delicate *objets d'art,* elegant and spirited trifles, or highly refined knick-knacks, although his terracottas were skilfully varnished and his few marble figures finely chiselled and charmingly decorative. The enchanting persuasiveness of his graceful *Madame Récamier,* whom he portrayed in several versions the best being that in the museum at Lyons, is not to everyone's taste. He also flirted with the theme of the Revolution (as in the medallion now in the Musée Carnavalet, Paris) making her appear more chic by giving her a profile like that of some haughty *ci-devant,* with her carefully studied hair-style crowned by a cap with a patriotic cockade somewhat similar to the magnificent ostrich plumes so dear to Marie-Antoinette.

For all his charm the elegant Chinard was in no way comparable to Canova, the finest·sculptor of the age, perhaps the last really universal Italian artist, and almost the counterpart in sculpture of David because of his influence on European art of the early 19th century. Magnificent testimonies to his close links with Napoleon and the Imperial family include the portraits of the Emperor that he executed at various times. That of 1808 is a heroically idealised Classical nude (the original marble version is in Apsley House, London, and the bronze replica in the courtyard of the Brera art gallery in Milan); another more human and perhaps more convincing portrait of the younger Bonaparte was studied from life during the artist's stay in Paris in 1802 (the original gesso model is at Possagno). His other sitters included Madame Mère, Murat, Caroline, Pauline, Cardinal Fesch and, of course, that tenth muse, Madame Récamier. But Canova does not really belong to this book since he always remained essentially Italian and was closer to Rome than to Paris.

An artist who was active in France during the Directoire, Consulate and Empire, and who died at the age of eighty-seven in 1828, was Jean-Antoine Houdon. Although he could not be said to be inferior to Canova, the fact remains that his later works never had the same complex and spontaneous elegance as

25   Pierre-Philippe Thomire (1751-1843). Bronze candel-abra. Musée Marmottan, Paris. A magnificent candelabra in chiselled gilded bronze with twenty-four branches and six small sculptures of seated sirens, made for the palace of the Infante. It later belonged to Hervas, Talleyrand and Baron A. de Rothschild.

26   Bronze sconce. Musée Marmottan, Paris. The decoration consists of a lion's head in gilded bronze crowned by palmettes and holding a bronze patera with three candle-holders. The sconce is of a rare design and dates from the late Empire period.

27   Pierre-Philippe Thomire (1751-1843). Gilded bronze statuette. National Collection of Fine Arts, Washington. The statuette, representing Summer, belonged to a large centre-piece. Centre-pieces (or *surtouts*) of the period were some-times as much as four yards long and usually consisted of different pieces including large arcaded trays lined with mirrors at the bottom.

28   Henri Auguste (born 1759). Silver soup tureen. Malmai-son. The tureen has a solemn, grandiose appearance inspired by antique forms, and was part of a *surtout* that was offered by the city of Paris to Napoleon for his coronation.

25   Pierre-Philippe Thomire (1751-1843). Bronze candel-abra. Musée Marmottan, Paris.

27 Pierre-Philippe Thomire (1751-1843). Gilded bronze
statuette. National Collection of Fine Arts, Washington.

65

28 Henri Auguste (born 1759). Silver soup tureen.
Malmaison.

those of the pre-Revolutionary period. Although he still sculpted with impeccable technical perfection there seems to be a lack of soul in such works as the icy bronze *Cicero* of 1804 (Bibliothèque Nationale, Paris) or the *Voltaire* in the Paris Panthéon – a far cry from the magnificent portrait of the philosopher which Houdon had sculpted many years earlier, which was a masterpiece of potentially romantic Neo-Classicism with its precarious balance between nature and artifice, striking realism and abstract idealisation. A work which belongs to his least creative period is the bust of the Empress Josephine (1808, Versailles), in which neither the diaphanous transparency of the marble, the exquisite modelling of each lock of hair or the glacial sumptuousness of the curves of her draperies succeed in giving life to her bloodless, pallid smile or the vacuous gravity of her splendid countenance. More expressive was the terracotta bust of Napoleon (Dijon Museum) which was his greatest achievement of the period and the only work that stands comparison with his wonderful portraits of the Ancien Régime. In this work there was a discreet hint of Antiquity in the studied but by no means pedantic carving of the features, ingeniously underlined by a ribbon running under the hair high above the broad forehead and flowing in cunningly calculated curves over the powerful neck. The sincerity and vehemence of the expression and its underlying impassioned firmness give the bust an unforgettable aura of generosity and virile power. The old artist must certainly have been conscious of his success when he signed his work: 'Sa Majesté l'Emp-

ereur et Roy, fait d'après nature, St Cloud, aoust
1806'.

Considerations of space forbid a description of the
activities of Francois Rude (1784-1855), whose
greatest works belong to the Romantic period, but
passing mention may be made of Denis-Antoine
Chaudet (1763-1810), the author of such works as
Cupid Catching a Butterfly (1802, Louvre), a sculpture
of such sterile, glacial formalism that it might well
justify the attacks made upon the Empire style by
detractors incapable of seeing anything in it but an
icy manifestation of an unnaturally funereal taste.
A similar judgement applies to Lemot (1772-1837)
and Cartellier (1757-1831), who were commissioned
together with Chaudet, Moitte (1746-1810) and
Roland (1746-1816) to decorate the outer wall of the
Louvre. Cartellier's well-known bas-relief *Glory
Distributing Wreaths* (1810) may have been appreciated by the occasional pedant, but its mechanical
symmetry and insipid composition wearies the eye
and recalls the uniformity of Nazi sculpture rather
than the golden rules of Classical compositions.
Moitte on the other hand, sometimes attained an
instant of genuine aesthetic emotion, as in his
Monument of General Desaix (1805, Hospice du
Grand Saint Bernard), in which the dying hero,
gently leaning against his horse, seems to be intoning
the finale of a grand opera rather than giving himself
up to religious reflections. Two or three fairly successful works were produced by F. J. Bosio (1768-
1845) such as the *Aristeus, God of Gardens* (1812,
Louvre) which according to Janneau 'ressortit à

l'aménité du XVIII siècle', and his fatuous *Henry IV as a Child* of a few years later, which Louis XVIII wished to keep permanently in his study. Under the Empire it was decided to execute a scheme which the Count of Angiviller had suggested many years before: to commission a series of sculptures of great men of the past. But the work was confined to mediocre artists like Moitte and Joseph Foucou who were a far cry from such sculptors as Pajou and Clodion.

The column of the Grande Armée in the Place Vendôme offered the sculptors the day a rare opportunity to display their talents, and Deseine, Boizot, Bosio and Bridan were some of the many artists who worked on its enormous bas-reliefs. A similar though less spectacular opportunity was afforded by the Panthéon and the Arch of the Carrousel. One of the artists who worked on the arch was Charles-Louis Corbet (1758-1808). More worthy of attention, however is his marvellous portrait of the young Bonaparte, a work still 18th-century in style but almost Romantic in spirit, with its suffusing note of sadness. It was one of the most beautiful and convincing sculptures of the dying century. The reproduction in this book is of the gesso model in the Invalides rather than the marble at Malmaison.

ARCHITECTURE

When Charles de Wailly (1729-98), the architect of the much admired Odéon theatre, was lying on his death bed, he cuttingly remarked 'In the salons of

29 Henri Auguste (born 1759). The Empress's sauce-boat. Malmaison.

30   Pierre-Philippe Thomire (1751-1843). Gilded bronze
amphora. National Collection of Fine Arts, Washington.

29   Henry Auguste (born 1759). The Empress's sauce-boat. Malmaison. This delightful object belonged to Josephine. It was made in 1803 and is splendidly chiselled in silver gilt. The three female figures are the three Graces.

30   Pierre-Philippe Thomire (1751-1843). Gilded bronze amphora. National Gallery of Fine Arts, Washington. The amphora has the exquisite workmanship characteristic of Thomire's creations. It was made into a candle-holder and belonged to a large centre-piece. Thomire's factory enjoyed amazing prosperity at the time and employed nearly eight hundred craftsmen.

31   Lyons silk. Malmaison. Thanks to Jacquart's technical discoveries and Camille Pernon's management, the Lyons silk factories enjoyed great artistic and commercial success under the Empire. The textile illustrated is decorated with elegant floral decorations, with one of the Empire's favourite motifs, two swans placed back to back in the centre.

31 Lyons silk. Malmaison.

modern Paris I see nothing but the tombs of ancient Romans or the new shops in the London streets. Before long French architecture will be inspired by the taste of lemonade sellers and fashion designers.' One of the most successful works of the first half of the Napoleonic period was the Arch of the Carrousel by Percier and Fontaine, official architects and arbiters of taste. But despite its charming polychrome marble, the grace of its proportions and its beautiful overall decorative effect (heightened by the bronze horses of St Mark's, which then crowned it), it had more of the fragility of an ornamental knick-knack than the triumphal severity of the work which had originally inspired it: the Arch of Septimius Severus at Rome. The architects of the Empire built much of the Paris we see today, such as the Rue de Rivoli: its long, covered arcades were built in a style that harmonised with Napoleon's solemn tastes. As Napoleon wrote in his memoirs at St Helena, he wished that 'Paris might become something fabulous, colossal, never-before-seen', and when he fought to have the architect P. A. Vigon's project for the Temple of Glory (now called the Madeleine) executed, he affirmed: 'It is a temple I want, not a church. A temple like those that existed in Athens but not at Paris'. His words echoed the grandiose Classicism which had already had supporters among architects of genius like Ledoux and Boullée who were now either dead or reduced to the by-no-means negligible role of theorists.

None of the new builders could compare in imagination or creative ability with the old masters, and credit for most original architectural creations must go to practitioners of the Ancien Régime.

It was J. F. Chalgrin (1739-1811), the architect of the famous Saint Phillippe-du-Roule (1768), who in 1807 designed the powerful Arc de Triomphe with its 'indispensable excess of solidity' that Quatremère de Quincy so greatly appreciated. The following year, A. T. Brongniart (1739-1813) began the building of the Paris Bourse, which he designed as a Classical temple crowned by a cupola and a great tympanum, the main body of the building being flanked by two enormous projecting wings to enclose the gigantic piazza destined for the factory. F. J. Belanger (1744-1812), the former architect to the Count of Artois, for whom he had built the enchanting Folie de Bagatelle (1777) which influenced the taste of an entire epoch, may have been the first architect to have used iron to cover the whole roof of a building when he built the Grain Market in 1808.

The use of iron as a building material was an important innovation and a veritable passion with Napoleon, who also wished to see the Temple of Glory built in iron. Six years before, the engineer Dillon had designed the first iron bridge outside England: the famous *passerelle* (foot-bridge) of the Louvre. The rate of building was intense and almost feverish in contrast to the early years of the Revolution, when Legrand (1743-1808) and Molinos (1743-1831) seemed mainly interested in dismantling the Bastille. Molinos completed the Marché Saint Honoré and soon afterwards, in 1811, became the architect of the Muséum. Four bridges were built across the Seine; the splendid arteries of the Rue de Castiglione and the Rue de la Paix were completed; the grandiose column in the Place Vendôme was erected with the aid of an army of sculptors; the former Palais Bourbon, which had become the seat of the Corps Legislatif, was altered and joined to the Hôtel de Lasay by means of a great portico. Other transformations of a similar nature were effected at the Luxembourg and the Palais Royal, not to speak of the Louvre where the parts added by Napoleon were perhaps equal in mass to all that had been built in the course of the centuries. Other, no less ambitious projects remained on paper, such as the amphitheatre-city that was to have been built on the Chaillot hill in honour of the King of Rome, and the proposed reconstructions at Versailles. (This would have been a disaster for French art if it is true that the plan included a proposal to knock down 'all those statues, in such bad taste' which people the splendid gardens.)

N. L. Durand (1760-1832) was the theoretician of the régime, and his declarations reveal that he was an heir of the great rationalists of the 18th century and a precursor of the modern functionalists: 'The object of architecture is utility. In a building we should follow those principles which ensure convenience, salubrity, solidity, commodity, symmetry and regularity; and they are also less costly.'

PORCELAIN

At the beginning of the Republican period there was a decline in porcelain production at Sèvres. As it had

32 Mahogany wash-stand. Malmaison.

33 *Guéridon* in Mahogany and gilded bronze. Musée
Marmottan, Paris.

34 Mahogany cheval-glass designed by Percier and made
by Jacob. Château of Compiègne.

32 Mahogany wash-stand. Malmaison. The form of an *athénienne*, here adapted for a wash-stand (*saut-de-lit*) was inspired by a famous painting by Vien. The present example, which dates from about 1802, recalls the famous tripod of the Temple of Isis at Pompeii. The basin and the jug are of Sèvres porcelain, the sphinxes of bronze.

33 *Guéridon* in mahogany and gilded bronze. Musée Marmottan, Paris. The *guéridon* reproduced here dates from the Empire period at its height. It is supported by colonnettes crowned with female busts with butterfly wings; the edge is decorated with finely worked bronze mounts and the white marble top with painted decorations. Above, a group of four graceful dancing girls of late 18th-century porcelain.

34 Mahogany cheval-glass designed by Percier and made by Jacob. Château of Compiègne. 'The frame is set at the base in the elegant counter-curve of the wings of the gilt sphinxes which flank it; they hold two feathered quivers of bronze arrows on their heads. Between the tendrils springing from the tails of the fabulous beasts which adorn the lunette at the base, the sneering head of the horned Pan.' (Comment by Mario Praz.)

35 Dressing-table in flecked elm. Malmaison. A work by the cabinet-maker Felix Remond, who furnished the Imperial household. It is designed rather like a console, with X-shaped legs decorated with superb bronze fittings. A swinging mirror supported like a cheval-glass by bronze supports shaped like candlesticks, is set on the white marble top.

35 Dressing table in flecked elm. Malmaison.

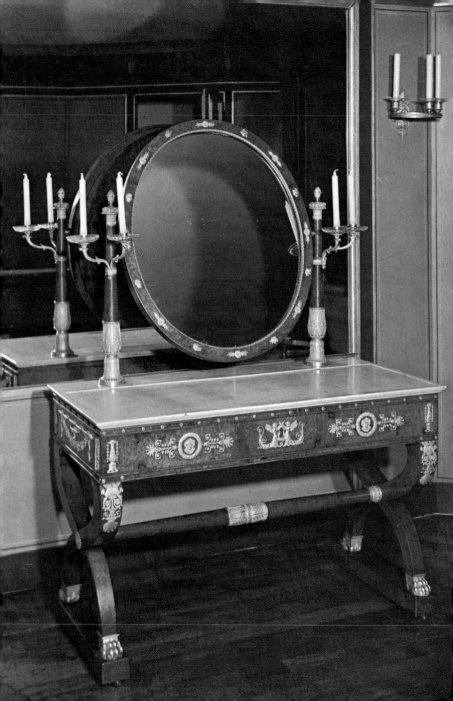

formerly catered for an essentially aristocratic client-èle, it was not easy to find a new market of equal importance in the new bourgeois class which was emerging into public life, even less so among the common people who were certainly not likely to throw away their savings on such luxurious trifles. But the crisis was of short duration and ended during the Convention, when the sculptor Boizot was again given the post of artistic director in which he had distinguished himself a few years before under Louis XVI.

Neo-Classical decorations were altered to conform to the taste of the day. Dinner sets were decorated with symbols of the Revolution instead of the former mythological and traditional floral themes. Coffee was served in delicate cups ornamented with Phrygian caps, lictors' fasces and tricolour flags (plate 21). Images of the goddess of Reason or Liberty, modelled after the beautiful citizen-actress Mademoiselle Aubry smiled with dignity from the sides of fine vases. Ceramic busts of heroes of the homeland began to be made, and the cold and hated features of Marie-Antoinette were replaced by those of Mirabeau, Marat and Robespierre.

During the Consulate, Napoleon gave the Director-ship of the factory to Alexandre Brongniart (1770-1847), the son of the famous architect, and the work produced under his inspiration completely changed the fortunes of the factory. Confident in his own scientific experience, which had embraced chemistry, geology and botany, he aimed to raise the technical quality of the wares. He was outstandingly successful, and some measure of his achievement may be seen in the gold decorations for porcelain whose surprising *ton sur ton* contrasts were obtained by combining mat and shiny gold patterns. One of his more surprising innovations was to suspend the manufacture of objects in soft clay, since they did not offer the same possibilities for easy modelling as kaolin. The result was the irremediable loss of that delicate plasticity that gave 18th-century porcelain so much of its charm.

Among the most impressive virtuoso pieces made at Sèvres was the famous Table of the Marshals now to be seen at Malmaison: it was made for his table top by the miniaturist Isabey, who designed a grandiose Sun-Napoleon glittering with the Byzantine pomp of his regal vestments and standing at the centre of thirteen radiating tongues of flame that ended in portraits of the Marshals of the Empire. The same solemn grace distinguished the great *pendule géographique* reproduced in plate 14. It was begun in 1813 but was still unfinished by the end of the Empire, when the projected head of Caesar was replaced by the twin heads of Diana and Apollo at the top of the exquisite herm designed by Fragonard the younger. The various movements of the hours in different parts of the planet (Paris, the Azores, Baffin Bay, California, Tahiti, Egypt and Persia) were illustrated in twelve medallions by the painter Develly.

Besides such works of direct political inspiration, and some repetitions of the so-called Etruscan style with fantastic transformations of Classical decorative themes and forms, a new taste arose for porcelain imitations of other materials such as jasper, porphyry, and especially bronze. Technicians and artists succeeded in imitating these materials with surprising success despite the protests of Percier and Fontaine, whose artistic authority was powerless to prevent the new development and who acrimoniously asked, 'What is the use of gilt covering all those vases? Do they wish us to believe they are made of gold. The fraud is badly applied here since gilded porcelain will never have the fineness and preciousness of gold. It thus loses its own merit without acquiring that of metal to the beholder.'

The fashion for 'Egyptian' objects was rampant, with everyone anxious to decorate his house with them. Napoleon himself placed an order at Sèvres for an enormous Egyptian table-piece (plate 18) which turned the centre of the table into a reconstruction of the most famous temples along the Nile. It is hard to imagine anyone eating a meal next to such a grandiose piece of stage scenery at least four yards long, but there is something moving in the literary enchantment which inspired this new kind of *ruinisme*. Words fail to describe the sugar bowl for the same dinner service: it was made in gold and blue enamelled porcelain covered with enigmatic hieroglyphics, the handle rearing arrogantly upwards like the menacing head of a cobra (plate 22).

Outside Sèvres there were several other porcelain factories in Paris, all producing wares of equal quality, for example those of Dihl, who in 1810 decorated a plate with an enchanting 'anticipated' portrait of the Imperial heir, who had not yet been born (plate 19). It was a kind of cherubic vision, with the child emerging out of the clouds against a background of

36   Bureau of the Empress Josephine. Malmaison.

37   Mahogany writing desk. Malmaison.

38 Mahogany *jardinière*. Malmaison.

36   Bureau of the Empress Josephine. Malmaison. A work signed by the brothers Jacob, who worked together from 1796 to 1803. The quality of their works was always high but here it is extraordinary, as can be seen from the perfect proportions and exquisite workmanship of every single ornamental detail. The writing desk was designed like a grandiose triumphal arch crowned by a golden frieze and sustained at the angles by winged Victories. The design was by Percier and Fontaine.

37   Mahogany writing desk. Malmaison. This bureau, dating from about 1805 was probably the work of the cabinet-maker C. Lemarchand. This has been deduced from a careful comparison with the console in plate 45 and an examination of the mounts on the central drawer, which are identical with others in works known to have been by his hand. The desk is surmounted by a set of drawers flanked by caryatids.

38   Mahogany *jardinière*. Malmaison. A small piece, of simple but refined design. It dates from about 1802 and belonged to Queen Hortense.

39   Library at Malmaison. Design by the architects Charles Percier (1764-1838) and Pierre Fontaine (1762-1853). 'The disposition of the site chosen for the building of this library necessitates its division into three parts and justifies the ordering of free-standing Doric columns to sustain intersecting arches. On one side you will find a glass-panelled door opening on to the garden path, and on the other a fireplace with a mirror facing the countryside. The medallions contain portraits of the most celebrated authors of Antiquity.'

39 Library at Malmaison. Designed by the architects
Charles Percier (1764-1838) and Pierre Fontaine (1762-
1853).

blue sky and surrounded by resplendent gold decoration in imitation of the rays of the sun.

Other marvellous objects were produced by Guerhard and Darte for the factory of Nast, and by the factory at Dagoty which furnished ceramics to the Empress Josephine and which produced a beautiful ink-stand as a gracious homage to the myth of Ganymede (Malmaison).

TEXTILES, WALLPAPER AND TAPESTRIES

Lyons remained the main centre of the textile industry during the Directoire and the Empire. By utilising Jacquart's important technical innovations, the leading local manufacturer, Camille Pernon, was able to increase production without lowering the outstanding quality of his textiles, which were now being used for covering walls as well as seats or curtains, since the fashion for wood-panelled interiors had died with the Ancien Régime.

One of the most popular materials was *lampas*, a flowered silk, for its lively sheen made a highly suitable background to the basic simplicity of the new furniture, its dark mahogany tones lightened only by bronze fittings or inlays of precious woods. The shades of silks had been clear and cool during the Directoire but they gradually became darker under the Empire. Decorations with such motifs as cameos, stars and bees alternated with solemn archaeological themes and the famous imperial 'N', destined to add a serenely aristocratic note to every interior 'we end up by quite liking all these N's and all these bees', as Proust's Duchess of Guermantes, despite her monarchical leaning remarked.

Those who could not afford Lyons silks decorated their homes with *toiles de Jouy*, which could still rely on graceful designs by J. B. Huet. He continued to design elegant cartoons until 1810, being inspired by the favourite literary and mythological themes of French society, the story of Paul and Virginie alternating with the myth of Cupid and Psyche and La Fontaine's charming fables. Similar textiles were still made at Rouen and Mulhouse and were printed with current motifs taken from the pattern-books most in fashion.

Although it was cheaper, wallpaper was in no way inferior to textiles with regard to decorative taste and elegance. The remains of the famous factory of Reveillon, destroyed in 1789, were quickly restored by Jacquemart. With great commercial acumen, he at once renewed his repertory of decorative patterns by having wallpaper printed with symbols of revolutionary liberties and even direct transcriptions of The Rights of Man or the articles of the Constitution. The manufacturer Dufour printed less political subjects on his wallpaper. The painter-decorator Laffitte provided him with delightful cartoons illustrating the story of Psyche in a delicate Prud'honesque style (the complete series has become rather rare but may be seen at the Musée Marmottan in Paris and at the villa of Marlia near Lucca); and Fragonard the younger composed charming scenes of the month of May.

Jean Zuber's factory was destined to enjoy greater

prosperity under the Restoration, and still exists today; but at this time it produced more exotic subjects, which corresponded to a prevailing pre-Romantic taste although they still echoed the Classical style. But the most striking change in wallpaper was when the long strips of friezes and the grotesques characteristic of Louis XVI interiors were replaced by panoramic views. Among the most important examples of the new manner are the *Scenes of the Revolution* dating from 1798 and the spacious views of the Gardens of Bagatelle dating from the beginning of the century – (source unknown). These panoramic views were framed by narrower strips imitating friezes or cloth draperies, and sometimes the simulation extended as far as entire *trompe l'oeil* linings which produced a very striking effect.

Despite Napoleon's patronage, the Gobelins factory did not distinguish itself artistically during this period. It continued to produce 18th-century subjects or to reproduce paintings by living artists such as David's *Brutus*, Regnault's *Liberty or Death*, Vincent's *Zeus* and, among other novelties destined to publicise Napoleon's feats, David's *Crossing of the Saint Bernard Pass* and Gros' *Plague Stricken Soldiers at Jaffa*. The administrator of the Imperial palaces continually ordered hundreds of coverings for chairs, foot-stools and divans, decorated with the predominant floral and Imperial motifs combined with stylistic reminders of the Louis XVI period.

Percier and Fontaine imposed their own decorative principles on Aubusson and provided designs for the famous *moquettes*. These, however, were inferior to the products of the Savonnerie: narrow woven carpets nearly half an inch deep, with beautiful clear pastel colours and designs by the decorator Saint Ange. The factory at Beauvais was managed by Huet, and made carpets in the style of the period. But they were neither technically nor artistically distinguished, though the firm enjoyed great prosperity.

BRONZES, SILVERWARE AND OBJETS D'ART

Throughout the period discussed in this book, French gold- and metal-work was dominated by Pierre-Philippe Thomire (1751-1843). A pupil of Gouthière, who decorated the exquisite interiors at Louveciennes for Madame du Barry, and of the sculptors Houdon and Pajou, Thomire had already won great fame under the Ancien Régime, as is proved by various works in which he collaborated. Among them were the splendid bronze garlands decorating the famous porcelain vases of Sèvres designed and executed by Boizot, and the finely chiselled bronzes ornamenting the *bureau plat* made by Beneman for Louis XVI at Versailles. After the inevitable crisis of the first Revolutionary period which ruined even the wealthy Gouthière, Thomire gradually attained a surprising degree of commercial prosperity, and when his career was at its peak he was employing as many as eight hundred workers in his factory.

40 Flecked mogany commode. Musée des Arts
Décoratifs, Paris.

41 Flecked mahogany *bonheur-du-jour*. Musée des Arts
Décoratifs, Paris.

40   Flecked mahogany commode. Musée des Arts Décoratifs, Paris. The work bears the stamp of C. Lemarchand, dates from between 1805 and 1810 and is a classic production of the Napoleonic era. The bronze mounts are of the very highest quality. The commode consists of four drawers, the topmost projecting over the others, flanked by caryatids, and it stands directly on the floor.

41   Flecked mahogany *bonheur du jour.* Musée des Arts Décoratifs, Paris. This piece came from the Hotel des Invalides and is certainly the work of C. Lemarchand. The bronze mount on the drawer is to be found on other pieces by the same cabinet-maker. The *bonheur-du-jour*, a kind of little feminine *secrétaire*, was especially popular under the Empire.

42   Armchairs in lacquer and gilded wood, designed by Percier and made by Jacob. Malmaison. The chair was one of the most beautiful models ever to come of Jacob's workshop and was designed as an armchair *en gondole.* Set in the curves of the back-piece are two white swans with long tapering wings and their thin necks richly inlaid with jewel-patterns. The Hellenic grace of the chair is heightened by the beautiful silk upholstery with a pattern repeating the swan theme.

43   Mahogany chair. Musée des Arts Décoratifs, Paris. The chair was designed so that officers might sit upon it with dignity without having to unbuckle their sabres. It was made at the beginning of the 19th century and is decorated with ivory inlays. The finely carved back has the same curve as that of the gondola chair. Note the curved back legs and the claw legs at the front.

42 Armchairs in lacquered and gilded wood, designed by
Percier and made by Jacob. Malmaison.

43   Mahogany chair. Musée des Arts décoratifs, Paris.

One of the many tokens of esteem he received was an invitation to dine with the First Consul, and once Napoleon had become Emperor it was only natural that Thomire should make some of his most splendid works for him. Apart from Marie-Louise's incredible *serre-bijoux*, in which he undoubtedly had a hand, one of his most spectacular works was the frieze of a nuptial procession on the great porcelain vase that the Sèvres factory dedicated to the new Imperial couple – a magnificent piece of work of perfect precision and lightness of touch. His decorations for the King of Rome's cradle (now at Vienna), for which the painter Prud'hon provided the design, became the model for all future royal babies' cradles – including, ironically enough that of the Bourbon Duke of Bordeaux, the posthumous heir of the Duke of Berry, who was to be greeted by the French Royalists as the 'son of the miracle'. So much did the 'life of forms' cut across political ideas. Two pairs of Classically proportioned cornucopias crossing in an 'X' formed the base for this exquisite object. Where they intersected they provided support for the winged youths keeping watch at the two ends of the thin, finely-worked cross-pieces holding the elliptical cradle, its dazzling series of silver-gilt decorations framing two lateral bas-reliefs with allegorical images of the Seine and the Tiber. It was surmounted by a canopy crowned by a winged Victory holding a laurel wreath. A fine mother-of-pearl tinted velvet awning was suspended from the wreath and (at the other end) the carved figure of a young eagle ready for flight – a magnificent testimony to Thomire's naturalistic virtuosity.

Given an artist capable of creating such a master-piece, it is impossible to forgive Marie-Louise's vandalism. In 1832, as Duchess of Parma, she ordered the splendid *Psyche* and the silver-gilt and lapis-lazuli dressing-table given her by the city of Paris on her marriage in 1810 to be melted down. The magnificence of such objects has to be imagined from the original designs of Thomire and Odiot (who was responsible for casting) and the water-colours of Prud'hon, who designed the composition. A wedding chest belonging to Marie Louise – almost certainly spared because it was in gilded wood – may still be seen at the Museo Glauco Lombardi at Parma; it too was probably designed by Prud'hon. The grace of the two winged female figures of Fame and History which hold up the coffer bring to mind a letter by the artist in which he accurately described the *Psyche* destined for the Hapsburg princess: 'the altar of Hymen is erected on the vase of Isis, emblem of the city of Paris, Tenderness and Fidelity, represented by doves, serve as bases. In the centre you will see two butterflies united to symbolise the union of souls. The altar sustains a column with a wreath of laurel en-twined around the base while a branch of ivy winds around it to show that numerous victims prepared the august alliance ... The whole is crowned by the figures of the God Mars and a young Minerva who are being joined together by Hymen. One Cupid leads the Austrian eagle on a leash of flowers while another caresses the French eagle ...'

That such a complex figurative programme with its exquisite Hellenising symbolism found a faithful interpreter in Thomire may be seen by other creations of the period, such as his famous *Table of the Marshals* at Malmaison, and the *Table of the Great Captains* at Buckingham Palace, by the side of which George IV an enthusiastic buyer and collector of Thomire's works, wished to have himself portrayed by Thomas Lawrence. Italy possesses one of Thomire's finest pieces of furniture in the great malachite table, crowned by a bronzed figure of Zephyr, which passed into the Stibbert Collection at Florence after having belonged to Jérome Bonaparte and Prince Anatole Demidoff, Princess Mathilde's husband.

A technical innovation had very important stylistic repercussions on the art of bronze and, more specifically, distinguished Thomire's Empire works from those he made under the Ancien Régime. Bronze works were no longer cast in a single piece but in a number of separate pieces which, when cold, were mounted together by means of nails and bolts after being patiently worked with a chisel. Such a process perhaps produced a rather colder impression, but it did result in technical perfection and allowed artists to indulge in new and highly fanciful decorative effects. One such was the superimposition of a matt finish on a shiny background, an inversion of the traditional order.

Also characteristic of the Empire period were pendulum-clocks, which were to be found on every mantelpiece and console and were sometimes accompanied by a set of candlesticks.

To make a profound study of all the stylistic variations, to follow every change as it occurred, would

44 Mahogany *secrétaire*. Malmaison.

45　Mahogany console. Malmaison.

44   Mahogany *secrétaire* Malmaison. The *secrétaire* was a luxurious piece of furniture that appeared frequently in Empire households. This piece dates from 1805 and consists of an upper section with a front flap that could be folded down, set on a base resembling a console, supported by caryatids or sphinxes (as is the case here) reflected in the mirror set between the back supports. *Secrétaires* were designed strictly for feminine use and were always finely executed.

45   Mahogany console. Malmaison. This console has the stamp of C. Lemarchand and came from the château of Saint Cloud, where it was once part of the Imperial furnishings. It is supported in front by two single-legged caryatids in wood painted to resemble bronze, and at the back by two plain pilasters framing a mirror as in the *secrétaire* in plate 44. It dates from about 1805.

46   Dressing table in yew. Musée des Arts Décoratifs, Paris. The piece is stamped by Jacob-Desmalter and almost certainly came from the Empress Josephine's boudoir in the Tuileries. Note the four lyre-shaped legs. The octagonal mirror is held between bronze candlesticks standing on the marble top.

47   Mahogany and bronze console. Praz Collection, Rome. The top consists of a beautiful mosaic of coloured marbles and is supported by a fillet decorated with finely executed bronze mounts (of a later period or, perhaps, different provenance) supported by four bronze claw legs surmounted by sphinxes – a very rare motif. The back pilasters frame a mirror. The clock is of French manufacture, dates from the Restoration, and is decorated with a portrait of Lord Byron.

46 Dressing table in yew. Musée des Arts Décoratifs, Paris.

demand many times the space available. Works might be graceful, charming or solemn, and maximum use was made of the decorative possibilities of bronze with gilt and exquisite patinas. Because such variety in style and treatment existed, works in metal provide a kind of conspectus of modes of being and feeling in the early nineteenth century.

It is interesting to note the extent to which works by outstanding artists of the time were absorbed and used in objects destined for essentially practical and decorative purposes, as had happened in the case of Gobelins tapestries and in some Sèvres ware. The *Princess Leopoldina Esterhazy*, a sculpture by Canova of the Princess painting, is to be found almost unchanged in a tiny gilded bronze on a clock in the Lefuel collection; David's young *Horatii* is repeated in little bronze figurines on another French clock, in the Royal Palace at Genoa, and on that in England, in the collection of Her Majesty The Queen. This popularisation of the major arts had some curious results under the Empire. When it was decided to extend to a wider public what had previously been jealously reserved for only the most aristocratic mansions, some French works of the period acquired – in spite of their notorious official air – a rather touching tone of intimacy without becoming vulgar or banal.

Mention has already been made of J. B. Odiot (1763-1850), one of the most highly esteemed metalworkers during the Empire period, and the creator of numerous works for Napoleon's palaces. His work is distinguished by its sobriety and technical accomplishment, although it sometimes contains a hint

47   Mahogany and bronze console. Praz Collection, Rome.

of grandiloquence. Such a charge could certainly not be levelled against Martin-Guillaume Biennais (died 1819). He set up a business in Paris in about 1800, at the 'Sign of the Violet Monkey', and provided the court with exquisitely designed and finished metal works as well as small furnishings, *nécessaires* and other *objets de vertu*. It was no accident that he was commissioned to make Napoleon's sword and other ceremonial apparel from designs by Percier and Fontaine. Some mention must be made of Henri Auguste (born 1759), who collaborated with Baron Denon to create some of the most elegant silver pieces of the period, such as the splendid sauce-boat (plate 29) in the dining room at Malmaison, which he made for the Empress. And there was a multitude of anonymous craftsmen who conferred the dignity of works of art on the characteristic *lampes bouillotte*, and on the oil lamps perfected by Quinquet (who gave them his name), which were made of plain, painted tin in the most varied and original shapes.

FURNITURE

'By restituting a multitude of objects which once were part of the interior furnishings and decorations of houses, the excavations of the cities of Herculaneum and Pompeii are furthering the taste for the imitation of the antique to an ever-increasing extent. Together with changes brought about in architecture, it all tends towards a reform of modern decoration; interlacing, contorted and irregular lines have become replaced by simple, pure lines and correct forms.' This observation was made in 1812 by Percier and Fontaine, and after their historical justification for the most recent developments in taste they went on to make a declaration of principles: 'In vain one would hope to find forms preferable to those the ancients have transmitted to us, whether in the art of the engineer or in the arts of decoration and industry. It is not that one should always attribute their superiority in every genre to the power of imagination or talent. But it seems to us that we may see the power of reason reigning in a great many parts, and reason is, to a greater degree than is commonly believed, the genius of architecture, ornamentation, and interior furnishing.' Such statements in the *Recueil de Décorations Intérieures* show the importance the authors gave to what they considered the evidence of the Greek rather than the Roman world, for they elevated its forms to the dignity of criteria on the basis of 'reason', taken in its 18th-century sense.

What appeared as the Empire style in furniture was a direct and natural development from the most advanced aspects of the last years of the monarchy. Late Louis XVI furnishing had assumed a chaste and austere character owing to the decisive influence of such artists as Hubert Robert (1733-1808) and J.-L. David. They took their inspiration from Antiquity for their designs for furniture that was beautifully made by Georges Jacob (1739-1814). The furniture which appeared in the *Loves of Paris and Helen* was already to be found in David's studio, and had already been carved in mahogany by Jacob from the artist's

48   Office chair in gilded wood. Malmaison.

49 Mahogany office chair. Malmaison.

48   Office chair in gilded wood. Malmaison. The form of this comfortable chair, with its slightly curved legs, resembles that of the gondola chair, especially because of its scroll-topped back. It is completely upholstered and has a removable cushion, thus resembling an 18th-century *bergère*.

49   Mahogany office chair. Malmaison. Once again the form of the back recalls a gondola chair. The strongly curved back was known as a back *en hemicycle.* The arm-rests are supported by winged, single-legged lions ending in claw feet and unlike many other chairs of the period, there is no division between the support of the arm-rest and the leg. The piece was made by Jacob in about 1805. An almost identical chair may be seen in a painting by Isabey of Napoleon in his study in the Tuileries.

50   Gilded wooden armchair. Malmaison. An example of a ceremonial chair of the late Empire. The back is flat and straight like that of an à *la Reine* chair of the 18th century and is topped by an arched pediment and flanked by two pilasters with Corinthian capitals. The upholstered arms are supported by winged lions ending, under a pedestal decorated with a daisy, in claw legs. The work dates from about 1810.

50   Gilded wooden arm-chair. Malmaison.

designs when the famous painting was completed for the King's brother in 1788. And some of Riesener's creations, such as the commode made in mahogany in 1775, and destined for the king's sojourns at Sèvres, already heralded the stark and basic simplicity of the Napoleonic style in the very choice of the wood used for it. The transition from Louis XVI to Directoire and Empire furniture should therefore be viewed in terms of an ideal, logical continuity rather than a revolutionary break. Although the Revolution of 1789 changed the destiny of France and Europe in many ways, it had only a slight influence on the leaders of the arts.

Consequently Louis Réau's statement that the Empire style was nothing more than an imperialistic phase of the Louis XVI style before becoming bourgeois under Louis Philippe is far-fetched. And similarly, the author can only disagree with Francis Watson's opinion that the Directoire and Empire styles differ from those of the Louis XVI period 'principally because of the inferiority of the execution and the materials used'. The soberly elegant furniture of the Empire certainly seems different from Louis XVI furniture but it is not necessarily inferior to it. What can be said is that it lost that vaguely perfumed air that the craftsmen of the Ancien Régime gave to their fanciful interpretations of Classical forms. Whereas in the past craftsmen made up for their lack of knowledge with imagination when interpreting the 'rational' forms of the Greeks, they now endeavoured to revive them with all the desperate precision of the philologist. But this does not mean that Empire furniture contained no element of poetic licence and was merely the product of a servile copying process, as many critics have wished to maintain. The categorical and unjust repudiation of Empire furnishings has begun to wane only in recent years; the reasons for its existence in the first place are unclear. The explanation does not lie in politics: from 1815 onwards, the restored monarchs enthusiastically decorated their palaces, ironically enough, with furniture that was clearly if not always strictly Napoleonic in style; and such furniture continued to be made until the middle of the century, when there was a mannered return to the 'Pompadour style'. Yet the Goncourt brothers, men of almost infallible artistic discernment, described the enchanting interior of Madame Récamier's room in the following terms: 'We are at number 7 in the Rue de Mont-Blanc. Mahogany rages throughout the room: mahogany pilasters, mahogany architraves and doors, mahogany window frames. Two gilded bronze swans surround the bed with a garland of flowers escaping from their beaks; the background to the bed consists of a mirror with a gold-filletted mahogany frame. But who lives in this mahogany gynaeceum? Who lives in the company of these gold-embroidered silk draperies and curtains of violet silk shot with black? Who can compose themselves to sleep between a mahogany night-table surmounted by a *corbeille* of tinplate flowers and another mahogany night-table with a gold antique lamp upon it? What woman is capable of dreaming in such a Pompeii, bordered on the left by a marble statue and on the right by a bronze candlestick?' We do not know why the Goncourts found this beautiful 'mahogany gynaeceum' so hateful. To us, these black- and gold-edged curtains, these finely worked antique-style bronzes, these pieces of furniture made of mahogany (a wood of rare elegance whose various tonalities and grains make it extremely attractive), and these swans holding a graceful garland of flowers do not appear in the least unpleasing. Taste is capricious. The Goncourts, who were the first to admire the gracefulness of the 18th century, refused to appreciate the less coquettish but no less appealing beauty of the Napoleonic style.

Let us examine the type of furniture that might have decorated a private house or a palace between the end of the 18th century and about 1815. Directoire chairs were often painted in clear colours, whereas they tended to be in dark wood or gilt under the Empire. To date them with a fair degree of exactitude, it is enough to examine the terminal part of the back, which began by curling in an 'S' before becoming straight. The backs of chairs and armchairs were often upholstered, though in other instances they were ornamented with elegant motifs in open-work, including a more stylised version of the Louis XVI lyre motif, balustrade themes and geometrical shapes elegantly composed into rhomboids, triangles and grilles. Another common type of chair back was a slightly S-shaped upholstered back whose top was in the form of an arched wooden cornice ending in a scroll. A characteristic of this period was the frequent joining of the back leg of a chair to the arm-rest with a single piece of wood carved in various styles. This

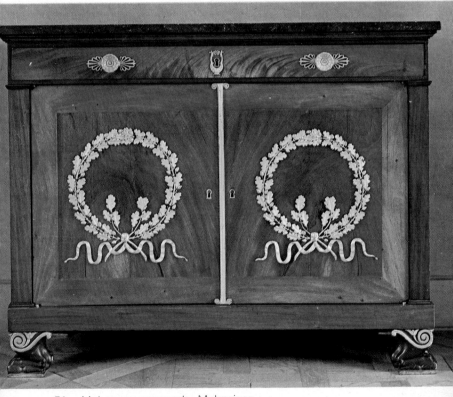

51 Mahogany commode. Malmaison.

52 Cradle ot the Duke of Bordeaux. Musée des Arts
Décoratifs, Paris.

53   Gilded wooden bed. Château of Compiègne.

51 Mahogany commode. Malmaison. The work almost certainly dates from the end of the Consulate or the first years of the Empire. The front consists of one visible drawer over two doors decorated with wreaths of oak leaves. The claw feet are set obliquely to the piece.

52 Cradle of the Duke of Bordeaux. Musée des Arts Décoratifs, Paris. This sumptuous cradle was made for the heir to the French throne in 1819 by the cabinet-maker Felix Rémond in collaboration with Desnière and Matelin who executed the rich bronze decoration. It is a heavier and rather over-pretentious version of the cradle of the King of Rome. It is an interesting example of the way the Restoration monarchy took over the Empire style.

53 Gilded wooden bed. Château of Compiègne. An official bed of the *en bateau* type made by Jacob-Desmalter in 1807. The balustrade elements that may be seen in the back part of the bed are to be found again in many Empire chairs and are identical with those in a series of armchairs made by the same cabinet-maker for Josephine two years later. The columns flanking the bed were intended to support a canopy.

54 Mahogany commode. Château of Fontainebleau. Like the *secrétaire* en suite in the same chateau, the commode was made after a design by Percier and Fontaine by the cabinet-maker G. Beneman. It is a compromise between the Louis XVI and early Empire styles, although not very successful: witness the indecisive disposition of the bronze decorations on the front.

54 Mahogany commode. Château of Fontainebleau.

leg-cum-arm-rest commonly had the form of a sheathed caryatid, a winged lion or a one-legged swan – frequently represented with spread wings so that the arm-rest had a wider support.

A type of seat that enjoyed great popularity during the Empire (and even after the Restoration) was the 'gondola seat' characterised by a back-piece sloping backwards and arm-rests that terminated abruptly and conferred a peculiar grace on the piece, especially when seen sideways. One particularly enchanting version of the gondola armchair was designed by Percier and Fontaine for Josephine at Malmaison. In addition to the features just described, it had two splendid white painted swans nestling in the space left free by the concave lines of the 'gondola' (plate 42). The front legs of this armchair are curved, which is rare for the period. The front legs of chairs were nearly always straight, though they might sometimes be claw-legged or decorated with spiral twists.

A very common type of seat under the Consulate and during the first years of the Empire was the curule type of chair in which the back legs, and sometimes the front as well, crossed in an 'X'. A rather curious design was that for the officer's chair in plate 43, its two short underarm-rests topped by shiny knobs and without any arm-pieces so that soldiers could sit in dignity on it without having to remove their sabres. Armchairs for the study or library were distinguished by their massiveness, their high and wide backs curving *en hemicycle*, and their leather upholstery (plate 49).

The *bergères* were a survival from the 18th century:

armchairs with a removable cushion and upholstered underarms and backs altered to fit the new taste. A new kind of seat was the so-called *causeuse*, simply a large armchair for two persons. Lastly, the *chauffeuse* was a particularly low chair designed for sitting close to a fire.

Divans were no longer particularly distinguished, for they simply appeared as much larger versions of armchairs or else were almost entirely upholstered and thus almost exclusively the work of the upholsterer. There was a special type of sofa, the *méridienne*, which had two ends of equal height (as in David's portrait of Madame Récamier) which were sometimes joined by a straight back-rest; when the two endpieces were of unequal height a backpiece would slope gracefully down from one to the other. Sometimes, for greater convenience, the lower end of of the *méridienne* could be folded down. The *duchesse* chaise-longue was rather less common, and although the example reproduced in plate 57 is not of particularly high quality it is interesting because of its rarity being a *duchesse brisée*, a chaise-longue in two parts. An old piece of furniture that reappeared in the imperial palaces was the stool, since Napoleon decided that armchairs were to be reserved only for the Empress and his mother. All the other members of the court, including the Princes of the Blood, had to sit on X-shaped stools which sometimes assumed highly ingenious shapes, for example that by Jacob-Desmalter in the Victoria and Albert Museum (originally from Saint-Cloud) with legs carved in the form of two crossed sabres. A very similar and equally elegant version was also made by a local craftsman for the Royal Palace at Naples.

The first beds to be produced after the fall of the monarchy were in the Louis XVI style, although they were now decorated with revolutionary symbols. One of the most important examples was the *à la Fédération* bed, the canopy supported by pilasters bearing lictors' fasces (a Republican symbol). A few years later the first *en bateau* bed made its appearance, being shaped in the form of a boat; one was made for Madame Récamier in 1798. The *lit à l'antique* had only one head-board, and like all Empire beds was placed lengthways against the wall.

But, contrary to the practice under Louis XVI, the bed now formed an integral part of the architecture of a room without ever being placed in an alcove. Sometimes a kind of little temple would be built around the bed, like that made by Percier and Fontaine (see plate 25 in their *Recueil*) for Monsieur O.'s room, a deliciously Classical extravaganza designed as a garden overflowing with greenery. There was a Hellenistic temple dedicated to Diana in the background amid antique vases and statues, and in the centre a splendid nuptial bed towered imposingly, flanked by winged single-legged lions. The Turkish bed, the type chosen by Monsieur O., had scroll-shaped ends, unlike the pulpit bed (*lit en chaire à prêcher*) reproduced in plate 59, which has straight ends. The so-called *lit à l'impériale* was simply a more sumptuous version of the pulpit bed.

The *console* was one of the *pièces de résistance* of Empire interiors. Narrow and elongated, it was

55 Mahogany pianoforte. Praz Collection, Rome.

56 Mahogany canapé. Musée Marmottan, Paris.

57 Mahogany chaise-longue. Praz Collection, Rome.

55 Mahogany pianoforte. Praz Collection, Rome. A work by Sébastien Erard, the famous early 19th-century maker of musical instruments. The pianoforte is decorated over the keyboard with an enchanting decoration in *verre églomisé* (painted glass incised with gold) in the style of A. Rescalon. To the right, a music-stand of the period.

56 Mahogany *canapé*. Musée Marmottan, Paris. The clean-cut architectural simplicity of the work indicates that it dates from the Directoire. The richness of the winged chimeras supporting the arm-rests appears forced by contrast with the plain straight back. The piece was made after a design by Percier and Fontaine which was repeated many years later in Italy by the Venetian G. Borsato.

57 Mahogany chaise-longue. Praz Collection, Rome. This type of seat, known as a *duchesse* or a *duchesse brisé* when composed of two pieces, resembles a lengthened version of a gondola chair with arm-rests supported by sphinxes. Such a model was very rare during the Empire, and was probably made by a provincial craftsman.

58 Mahogany stool. Musée Marmottan, Paris. This X-shaped stool with claw legs topped by lions' heads was part of the furniture of the three Consuls in the Tuileries. It was made by the brothers Jacob, who worked together from 1796 to 1803, and dates from the beginning of the century.

59 Mahogany bed. Musée Marmottan, Paris. Originally Napoleon's bed in the Imperial Palace at Bordeaux. It was of the *chaire a prêcher* (pulpit) type, with straight ends decorated with sculpted female heads and vases. The bronze decorations are by Thomire.

58   Mahogany stool. Musée Marmottan, Paris.

usually rectangular in shape, the front legs usually carved in fantastic zoomorphic designs and the back legs shaped as coupled pilasters which, in the more expensive pieces, held a mirror reflecting the front legs to make the piece appear twice its size. There were some exceptions, for example the exquisite console in the Praz collection (plate 47) with its four claw-legs surmounted with little sphinxes – a motif derived from Ancient Roman furniture which sometimes reappeared in a piece of Neo-Classical furniture. Consoles were sometimes semi-circular; very occasionally two consoles joined together to resemble a normal rectangular or square table would be set in the centre of a room. Consoles were always show-pieces and were particularly refined in execution when they were made for an important household. They were frequently decorated with finely worked bronze *mounts*, porcelain plaques and coloured marble tops.

Another equally luxurious piece of furniture was the *guéridon*, a little circular table with three legs (like that in the Musée Marmottan reproduced in plate 33) or, more usually, a central support ending in three short claw legs. The top could often be rotated for greater convenience, as for example when taking tea. Such small pieces were often creations of bronze- and marble-workers rather than of furniture-makers, and were made with the most precious materials. A knick-knack which the Empire inherited from the Monarchy was the *athénienne*, which first made its appearance in 1763 when the painter Vien exhibited a painting at the Salon which featured an elegant incense burner on a tripod. At Malmaison

Josephine owned an *athénienne* (plate 32) which was used as a *saut-de-lit*, a small wash-stand provided with a small basin and a porcelain jug. It is worth noting that even this piece of furniture had claw legs topped with sphinxes, like the console in the Praz collection. The iron and bronze *athénienne* reproduced in plate 66 was intended as an incense-burner, and a water-colour by Percier and Fontaine in the Lefuel collection (plate 67) shows a bed flanked by two *athéniennes* used as *jardinières*. But all *jardinières* were not *athéniennes*, as may be seen from the mahogany example in plate 38, with its simple but elegant lines and with gilded bronze mounts as its only decoration. It was once part of the furnishings of Queen Hortense's private mansion in the Rue Cerutti and is now to be seen in the Empress's home at Malmaison. A rarer piece resembling the *athénienne* was the *lavabo imperial*. According to Grand-jean only a few specimens have survived, including that built for Napoelon in 1809 by Jacob-Desmalter (now at Compiègne). Instead of standing on three legs like an *athénienne*, the *lavabo* has four claw legs decorated at the top with gilded female heads.

Small pieces of furniture remained much the same as they had been under the Bourbon monarchs. One of the most important was perhaps the *serre-papiers* or paper-holder, designed in the shape of a small funerary urn mounted on arched claw legs and decorated with good quality bronze mounts. Its place was in the library, next to the writing desk; but given its modest size it may be asked whether it really served any useful purpose. The most elegant specimen I know is that by Biennais at Malmaison (it may be seen in the background, behind the *guéridon*, in plate 39), but another fairly elegant pair is in Caroline Murat's study at Naples.

Small tables did not compare in quality with the more varied designs of the 18th century. One of the most successful was a work table which could also be used as a *poudreuse* or writing table. The top could be folded back to reveal a mirror and a narrow drawer. The table stood on cross legs joined by a carved cross-piece. It had a fragile air appropriate to the intimacy of a feminine boudoir, where it would be accompanied by a large *toilette* (dressing table), a piece of furniture that had only recently made its appearance in French interiors.

In the 18th century, *toilettes* were simply tables that had been covered with a cloth, but they now tended to resemble a console with the addition of a medium-sized mirror supported by two pivots. One of the most beautiful examples to survive is that from the Tuileries, reproduced in plate 46. It is carved in yew and, delicately decorated with chiselled and gilded bronze, stands on four lyre-shaped legs and supports an octagonal mirror held by two candlesticks. The elm *toilette* at Malmaison (plate 35) had cross legs and an oval mirror covered with beautiful bronze mounts. As already mentioned, the most elegant of these *toilettes* was melted down a hundred and thirty years ago by Marie-Louise in order to alleviate the sufferings of the population of Parma, which had been stricken by a severe cholera epidemic – a strange destiny for a piece of furniture which had been speci-

59   Mahogany bed. Musée Marmottan, Paris.

60   Dining room at Malmaison. The wall decorations were inspired by Pompeian frescoes and give a graceful touch to the interior, which is in the style of the Consulate period. The round table is surrounded by chairs in the style of the Directoire (note the typical S-shaped backs) to which Josephine always remained faithful.

61   Flecked mahogany *secrétaire*. Royal Palace, Naples. A high-quality piece of furniture which may be compared with Josephine's *secrétaire* at Fontainebleau, as Grandjean has remarked. It is decorated with superb bronze mounts, that in the centre, representing Wisdom keeping Cupid away from a Young Girl, is to be found again, minus the right-hand figure, on Lemarchand's commode, reproduced in plate 40.

62   Flecked mahogany commode. Royal Palace, Naples. Like the *secrétaire* in the previous plate, the commode belonged to Caroline Murat, Queen of Naples. The central mount, representing a Poet on a Couch Crowned by a Winged Genius, is to be found again on a drawing-room organ reproduced in plate 77 of Brunhammer's book. The other mounts — Dancing Girls inspired by Pompeian frescoes — reappear, identical in form, in Queen Hortense's jewel-case, a work by Adam Weisweiler, now in the Napoleonsmuseum at Arenenberg.

60   Dining room at Malmaison.

61 *Secrétaire* in flecked mahogany. Royal Palace, Naples.

62   Commode in flecked mahogany. Royal Palace, Naples.

fically designed and dedicated to human vanity!

The *somno* was a little table in the shape of a truncated pyramid or, more often, of a parallelepiped. In Italy, however, it was usually cylinder-shaped. As its name indicates, it stood next to a bed. It was almost always made of mahogany or the same wood as the bed, and the front would be decorated with allegorical bronzes or learned inscriptions, sometimes even in Greek. It was topped by a marble slab.

Apart from the types already listed, there were of course the gaming tables inherited from the 18th century, which were adapted to conform to the archaeologically minded taste of the period; and there were many ingenious variants on the convenient small tables of the Ancien Régime such as the *vide-poche, tricoteuses* and *tables à la Tronchin*.

Dining tables had now become frequent, and were often oval or round in shape, like that in the dining room at Malmaison. The great tables for libraries or other uses repeated the form of the *guéridon*. One of the most famous specimens is the enormous table in the Grand Trianon by the cabinet-maker Felix Rémond. This was designed in a strict Empire style, though it was made in 1823, its enormous teak top resting on six massive elm sphinxes standing back-to-back.

The *psyche* or cheval-glass was undoubtedly one of the greatest inventions of 19th-century furniture-makers. Its design resulted from the greater size that mirrors were beginning to assume after having been very expensive and only of limited dimensions. Once they had become more common, they were poised between two high wooden side supports – as may be seen in the *toilettes* to which the *psyche* was closely related – and set on a solid base on the floor which made it possible to move the mirror about as one wished. Although it was usually rectangular, the *psyche* could also be oval, like the example reproduced here (plate 34) with its beautiful outward-facing sphinxes and, as usual, two candle-holders of medium height.

The commode no longer had the great variety of forms that characterised it in the Louis XVI period. There were two main types: those with three or four drawers (plate 40) and those with two or three doors to hide the drawers (plates 51 and 54). Some historians have seen an English influence in this last type of commode (also called *bas d'armoire*), since French examples are only to be found from the beginning of the Neo-Classical period. The front of the commode was often flanked by two small projecting columns or two pilasters or by sphinxes or caryatids; and they were decorated with gilded bronzes which might feature the most varied mythological themes or simple lions' heads on the handles. In the commodes with drawer divisions the upper drawer often projected above the others to emphasise the architectural composition of the front.

The first Directoire-Empire-style commodes were hardly different from early models: the commode designed by Percier and Fontaine and executed by Beneman (plate 54), for example, is a curious and not altogether happy union of the more delicate forms of the Louis XVI period with what was to be the pon-

63   Chair in mahogany and satin-upholstered wood.
Malmaison.

64   Mahogany writing desk. Musée Marmottan.

63 Chair in mahogany and satin-upholstered wood. Malmaison. A chair with the mark of the brothers Jacob and dating from about 1800. It is decorated with ebony inlays and pewter dots. The back is gracefully S-shaped, as in Directoire chairs to form a counterpoint to the curved back legs. Note the balustrade elements in the back.

64 Mahogany writing-desk. Musée Marmottan, Paris. The wide desk top has an edge decorated with green bronze patera, and rests on eight winged lions sculpted in mahogany. The work was certainly by Pierre Antoine Bellangé. The porcelain vases are an imitation of porphyry and the beautiful bronze 'Egyptian' ink-stand features a slave between two winged gryphons.

65 Mahogany writing desk. Pitti Palace, Florence. Various examples of this ingenious writing desk still survive. This one was designed by the Tuscan cabinet-maker Socci for Princess Elisa Baciocchi in about 1810. That at Malmaison was given by her to Napoleon.

66 Iron and bronze *athénienne*. Malmaison. This graceful tripod was inspired by the ancient bronzes of Pompeii, of which it is almost a direct copy. It owed its French name of *athénienne* to a painting by Vien entitled *La Vertueuse Athénienne* in which it made its first appearance. The example illustrated was used as an incense-burner.

65 Mahogany writing desk. Pitti Palace, Florence.

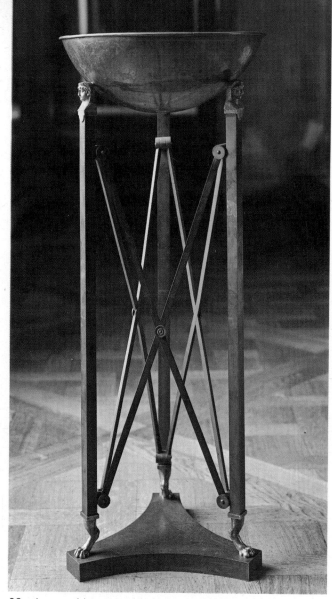

66 Iron and bronze *athénienne*. Malmaison.

derous ornamental style of the Empire in its heyday.

Chiffonniers consisted of various superimposed drawers, and were always pieces of great utility but rarely of any great decorative value. They were also known as *semainiers*. *Secrétaires à abattant* were tall and narrow in shape, had an upper section with a folding flap and were supported by drawers (as in the fine mahogany and lime-wood model that belonged to Cambacérès and is now in the Chantrell Collection) or else by two doors which concealed drawers and shelves. An even more refined type of *secrétaire* was supported by a kind of console with wood carvings reflected by the mirror at the back, as were the legs of the person sitting at it. One of the most beautiful examples of this type is the one that belonged to Caroline Murat (plate 61). It is decorated with bronzes of superb quality, and it is interesting to note that the exquisite bronze mount decorating the folding flap on the exterior is to be found, minus the right-hand figure only, on Lemarchand's commode (plate 40), now in the Musée des Arts Décoratifs in Paris. The same gilded bronze ornaments would often appear on different pieces of furniture, as in various works by Lemarchand all decorated with a mount of two winged figures flanking an altar and holding lions on leashes (plates 37, 41 and 45).

The *bonheur-du-jour* had enjoyed great favour under Louis XV. It still retained a certain popularity, although it was no longer identical to its 18th-century prototype: it now closely resembled a *secrétaire à abattant*, from which it differed only in having smaller dimensions and a base like a console. The roll-topped *secrétaire* was no longer fashionable, though plates 20 and 32 in Percier and Fontaine's *Recueil* show designs for this piece of furniture. They were brought up to date and designed in the Napoleonic style, but neither piece is attractive, the one because of its heavy official air, the other because of its excessive and over-elaborate decoration. More successful and typical of the Empire style were the *bureaux plats*, writing tables which, when of high quality, were often supported by bronze caryatids or sphinxes. One of these beautiful tables belonged to Caroline Murat and may be seen at Naples. Its sphinxes bear a strong resemblance to those on the two consoles now at Saint-Cloud and the Grand Trianon, although they lack wings. A *bureau plat* might sometimes be surmounted by a *cartonnier* (plate 37), a series of hide covered containers inserted in variously ornamented wooden frames. A very common type of writing desk consisted of a large top supported by two solid lateral sets of drawers at the sides and decorated at the corners with caryatids, one-legged lions and other examples of the decorative fauna of the Empire. This was Napoleon's favourite type of writing desk, and he was painted standing next to one in the painting by David already mentioned. The desk may still be seen at Fontainebleau and is one of Jacob-Desmalter's finest works. The top of this kind of writing desk opened with a spring. Sometimes the bureau or writing table took on the appearance of a triumphal arch when made for some luxurious interior; the greatest example of its kind is reproduced in plate 36. It belonged to Josephine and was a veritable triumph of the bronze-gilder and cabinet-maker's art, with a magnificent frieze, winged Victories that round off the corners, and a grandiose architectural aspect.

Two curious types of writing desk were made at different times for Napoleon. The first, in steel, gilded bronze and mahogany, might almost be a piece of contemporary furniture because of its basic and clean-cut design. It was designed as a kind of travelling case to be placed on a removable metallic base and divided into two small table tops, the forward part folding down to form a writing surface. It was made for the young Napoleon towards the end of the 18th century, and it can be seen in the Musée des Arts Décoratifs at Paris. The second (plate 65) was designed in 1807 by an Italian, the Florentine cabinet-maker Giovanni Socci, who for a long time worked for the Emperor's sister, Elisa Baciocchi. This piece looks like an oval scuttle resting on six claw legs with symmetrical dividing pilasters surmounted with lions' heads; a seventh leg ends in a gilt internode which is one of the three legs of a chair which can be easily removed from the table. The piece can then be opened up to form a desk with a writing surface and a compartment with little drawers. This ingenious design was so popular that various copies were made of it, including two now in the Pitti Palace in Florence, another at Malmaison and a fourth that was recently sold at a London auction.

Finally, it should be noted that Empire book-cases were often made as independent pieces of furniture.

67   Charles Percier (1764-1838) and Pierre Fontaine (1762-1853). Design for a bed-chamber. Lefuel Collection, Paris. Like the walls, the bed is draped in blue and is set on a raised platform with two bronze *athéniennes*. Two high and slender columns topped by statues support a canopy with curtains opening to disclose a large mirror. The elegant symmetry of the composition is completed by two armchairs and two chests of drawers.

68   Mahogany armchair. Musée des Arts Décoratifs, Paris. The chair dates from the beginning of the 19th century and has the Classic appearance of a curule's chair. The back legs are curved instead of being crossed like the front legs, as in other designs.

69   Mahogany occasional table. Musée des Arts Décoratifs, Paris. This small piece, known as an *en cas* table, served various purposes, and the handles at the sides made it easily carried. It dates from the beginning of the Empire period.

70   The Empress Josephine's bed-chamber at Malmaison. The grandiose gilded bed with its extremely elegant ornamental motifs – such as the winged swans and the cornucopias shaped like the initial 'J' of the Empress – was the work of Jacob-Desmalter (1810). On the little work-table at the right is a shield-shaped mirror like a miniature cheval-glass, made by the cabinet-maker Biennais. Apart from the sumptuous harmony of the white, red and gold decorations of the room which was designed as a tent, note the mirror placed directly behind the bed, a frequent practice from the Directoire period onwards.

67   Charles Percier (1764-1838) and Pierre Fontaine
(1762-1853). Design for a bed-chamber. Lefuel Collection,
Paris.

68   Mahogany armchair. Musée des Arts Décoratifs, Paris.

69 Mahogany occasional table. Musée des Arts Décoratifs Paris.

Percier and Fontaine designed one in the Egyptian style; another that recalled the design of a *bonheur-de-jour* belonged to Queen Hortense at Arenenberg; and one in violet wood was one of Marie Louise's favourite pieces at Compiègne.

This brief survey of the most common types of Napoleonic furniture would be incomplete without some mention of Sebastien Erard's beautiful musical instruments, in particular, the harps and pianofortes. The pianoforte illustrated in plate 55, and those at Malmaison and in the Royal Palace at Amsterdam, once belonged to Queen Hortense. Antoine Rascalon decorated them with plaques of *verre églomisé* (painted and gold-inlaid glass).

It must be admitted that the Empire style lacked the delicate poetry of the early Neo-Classical period, when the recent rediscovery of Antiquity fired the minds of artists to reconstruct its forms freely as they thought fit. But it still produced furnishings with a noble dignity of their own, and an elegant grace which avoided affectation and sometimes gave an effect of warm intimacy to interiors. When it was of good quality, French Empire furniture was always severely restrained, solid but not oppressive, well proportioned and never vulgar. A certain literary element and a tendency towards abstract forms gave it an aristocratic character which never degenerated into pretentiousness. The Empire was the last great style to appeal to the delicate sensibilities of aesthetes while still satisfying certain bourgeois tastes, and it was no accident that the *fin de siècle* decadents were the first to rediscover and appreciate its basic forms

70   The Empress Josephine's bed-chamber at Malmaison.

after more than half a century of neglect and scorn.

After the Louis XIV period, no other furniture was as grandiose and solemn, as rich and aristocratic as that of the Empire. Interiors had both the cold splendour of an Egyptian tomb and the sumptuousness of Byzantium. But it should not be forgotten that the furniture of this period was developing in two different directions: one towards the heroic and rhetorical style, the other towards an atmosphere of calm, restraint and privacy. The first was represented by bronze decorations, gold, and vast surfaces of darkly shining mahogany; the second by discreet inlay work, bronze fittings and the occasional use of the warmer tints of European woods. Although the King of Spain had an entire room decorated in platinum, although the Empress slept in a gilt nuptial bed led by gold swans and supported by gold cornucopias, and although Baron Denon wanted silver inlays for the Egyptian statues in his alcove, the Empire style survived such extravagances. Its rationally designed interiors, its feeling for space and decoration, and the principles laid down by the Imperial decorators are still valid today. If we forget the peremptory tone in which these principles were first uttered, we shall find that they are still capable of giving a touch of civilised humanity to the square boxes in which we are now obliged to spend our lives.

LIST OF ILLUSTRATIONS   Page